EMPOWERING LATINA NARRATIVES

MARGARET CANTÚ-SÁNCHEZ

EMPOWERING LATINA NARRATIVES

Navigating the Education/Educación Conflict in the Third Space

THE UNIVERSITY OF
ARIZONA PRESS
TUCSON

The University of Arizona Press
www.uapress.arizona.edu

We respectfully acknowledge the University of Arizona is on the land and territories of Indigenous peoples. Today, Arizona is home to twenty-two federally recognized tribes, with Tucson being home to the O'odham and the Yaqui. Committed to diversity and inclusion, the University strives to build sustainable relationships with sovereign Native Nations and Indigenous communities through education offerings, partnerships, and community service.

© 2025 by The Arizona Board of Regents
All rights reserved. Published 2025

ISBN-13: 978-0-8165-5477-5 (hardcover)
ISBN-13: 978-0-8165-5476-8 (paperback)
ISBN-13: 978-0-8165-5478-2 (ebook)

Cover design by Leigh McDonald
Typeset by Leigh McDonald in Arno Pro 11/14, Alternate Gothic No. 1 D, and Cheddar Gothic Rough (display)

Publication of this book is made possible in part by the proceeds of a permanent endowment created with the assistance of a Challenge Grant from the National Endowment for the Humanities, a federal agency.

Library of Congress Cataloging-in-Publication Data
Names: Cantú-Sánchez, Margaret, 1984– author.
Title: Empowering Latina narratives : navigating the education/educación conflict in the third space / Margaret Cantú-Sánchez.
Description: Tucson : University of Arizona Press, 2025. | Includes bibliographical references and index.
Identifiers: LCCN 2024032658 (print) | LCCN 2024032659 (ebook) | ISBN 9780816554775 (hardcover) | ISBN 9780816554768 (paperback) | ISBN 9780816554782 (ebook)
Subjects: LCSH: Hispanic American women—Education. | Mexican American women—Education. | Hispanic Americans—Ethnic identity. | Mexican Americans—Ethnic identity. | Discrimination in education—United States.
Classification: LCC LC2670 .C365 2025 (print) | LCC LC2670 (ebook) | DDC 371.822089/68073—dc23/eng/20241211
LC record available at https://lccn.loc.gov/2024032658
LC ebook record available at https://lccn.loc.gov/2024032659

Printed in the United States of America
♾ This paper meets the requirements of ANSI/NISO Z39.48-1992 (Permanence of Paper).

*This book is dedicated to the educators of our
cultures, homes, and schools—thank you.
To students everywhere, always remember
your voices and stories have power.
To my children, Mario Jesús and Carolina Inés,
may you always remember where you come from.
To my grandparents, Esther and Alfonso and
Margarita and Enrique, thank you for paving the way.*

CONTENTS

	Acknowledgments	ix
	Introduction: Balancing Grandma's Kitchen *Educación* and Academics in the Third Space of Education	3
1.	Contextualizing the Education/Educación Conflict Within the History of Latinx Education	21
2.	Problematizing the U.S. Education System and Its Impact on Latina Identity, Epistemologies, and Family	52
3.	Navigating the Education/Educación Conflict in *Golondrina, Why Did You Leave Me?*	79
4.	The Education/Educación Conflict in Academia: Reconciling Academic and Cultural Epistemologies in Latina Testimonios	98
5.	*Ni de aquí, ni de allá*: Contending with the Education/ Educación Conflict and Transforming the Classroom into the Third Space of Education	128
	Bibliography	147
	Index	155

ACKNOWLEDGMENTS

I want to thank my family, especially my husband, Jesús J. Sánchez, for their endless support and encouragement. This work would not have been possible without you. Thank you for always having my back. Thank you to my mentors who offered original comments on this manuscript when it was in its dissertation form: Drs. Cantú, Saldívar-Hull, Rendón, and Portillo. Thank you to the scholars and writers of the Comadrehood of Writing group for inspiring me to return to this research and prepare it for the world. Thank you to the reviewers for offering their feedback. To Kristen Buckles, editor extraordinaire, thank you for believing in me and this manuscript. Lastly, thank you to my colleagues at St. Mary's University; your support means the world to me.

EMPOWERING LATINA NARRATIVES

INTRODUCTION

Balancing Grandma's Kitchen Educación and Academics in the Third Space of Education

Grandma's kitchen was my first classroom, where I learned about who I am and where I come from, and as I reflect on those lessons, I realize they helped shape who I would become. As my first mentor and role model, my grandmother passed along the *educación* of our culture, including advice on how to be a strong, independent, educated woman. She served as my family's *maestra* (teacher), teaching my mother and aunts how to intricately weave educación and education together just as she did with the thread and cloth she used to make each of her grandchildren's blankets. For my grandmother, the educación of our home was just as important as the education received at school. Thus, because of Grandma's insistence, all five of her children attained college degrees, including my mother, who encouraged my brother and me to do the same. I took my mother's and grandmother's lessons to heart, working hard to attain my academic goals and eventually becoming the first in my family to achieve a doctoral degree.

As I began my journey through academia, I discovered that much of the Latina/Chicana literature I encountered focused on the theme of conflicting identities, which I attributed to the oppositional epistemologies encountered at school and at home due to assimilation. Though I initially began this research more than ten years ago with the hopes of exploring how Latina/Chicana students deal with these conflicting identities and epistemologies,

I find that this issue continues to be a relevant one, as evidenced by, among other discriminatory laws, the laws currently being passed across the United States and the culture wars enacted in our schools through the banning and censorship of books. Thus, I return to this question of whether we can balance divergent epistemologies; it is a question I pose to my students every semester, with varying responses each year. In the time since I originally began this research, much has happened, including the rise of the Black Lives Matter and #MeToo movements, the election of Trump, and a worldwide pandemic. These global changes have forced a need to reconcile and adapt strategies to balance cultural educación with formal schooling. Though my initial reflections on this questioning of identity began with my academic journey into higher education, in the years since, I have considered how these identity issues emerge among my students, in literature, throughout history, and as the world continues to undergo significant social changes.

Some of those impactful societal changes, including social unrest, political division, and the resurgence and retraction of antiracist scholarship and activism, among others, have become exacerbated by a global pandemic due to the COVID-19 virus. Although COVID-19 emerged five years ago, none of the other global changes I witnessed during my time in academia as an English professor have produced effects as profound as those we continue to see because of the pandemic. Especially problematic is the fact that though humanity seemed to come together in our shared time of need during the pandemic, we as a society failed to address the racial inequities that were brought to light because of it, including the digital divide, racial health disparities, and violence enacted against black and brown men by police.[1] Though many people began to recognize the existence of systemic racism as the world watched the murder of George Floyd on our screens and thousands flocked to protest it despite

---

1. It is important to note that the murder of George Floyd by police officers reignited the Black Lives Matter movement; this movement, however, originally began in 2013 with three female black organizers—Alicia Garza, Patrisse Cullors, and Ayọ Tometi. Black Lives Matter began with a social media hashtag, #BlackLivesMatter, after the acquittal of George Zimmerman in the shooting death of Trayvon Martin back in 2012. The movement grew nationally in 2014 after the deaths of Michael Brown in Missouri and Eric Garner in New York. Furthermore, even before this specific movement many activists and others called out the systemic racism of police forces that often discriminate against black and brown men.

the pandemic, society quickly forgot what groups such as Black Lives Matter, the We Are Here movement, and various NAACP chapters had been protesting in the first place, at that time and for decades before that.[2] In many ways, it seems that since that time of social unrest, divisions have been sown and reaped globally, especially in the United States, resulting in discriminatory and blatantly racist laws reminiscent of the Jim Crow era. Such disparities existed long before George Floyd. Still, the pandemic highlighted these inequities and allowed society to contemplate those injustices that existed beyond the streets and inside classrooms.

After the pandemic, rather than take the time to consider why teachers are overworked; why there is a mistrust of the health care system, especially among people of color; and why we continue to discriminate against minorities such as LGBTQIA+ and BIPOC individuals, society has willfully chosen to return to our racist and discriminatory origins.[3] Especially problematic are the laws passed in my home state of Texas and in Florida, including bills that criminalize and ban drag performances, prohibit gender-affirming care for teenagers and adults, and ban DEI (diversity, equity, and inclusion) programs in universities. Most telling is the banning and outright censorship of books by and about BIPOC and LGBTQIA+ individuals as well as those that discuss racial discrimination and racism. As a professor of Latinx/Chicanx literature, when it comes to the censorship of books that I specifically research, study, and utilize in classes on Mexican American literature, multiethnic literature, Latinx literature, and more, I am not surprised by these decisions made by

---

2. The We Are Here movement was developed by singer Alicia Keys and others to address the inequities present in our world. The movement calls on people to make a more just and equitable world.

3. The term *BIPOC* stands for "black, Indigenous, and people of color" and in recent years has become the term utilized to describe minorities of color in the United States. I use this term when discussing the discrimination faced by many minorities of color in the United States, but I also recognize that their experiences, histories, and identities are diverse and nuanced. I utilize the term *LGBTQIA+* to refer to those who identify as lesbian, gay, bisexual, transgender, questioning/queer, intersex, asexual, and more. I use this term to recognize those individuals who use these terms and to express my solidarity with them.

lawmakers in Texas because discrimination against BIPOC students has long been ingrained in Texas's and the United States' education history.[4]

For someone who teaches and researches Latinx/Chicanx literature and cultural studies, these laws come as no shock; in fact, the history of the U.S. education system reveals an ongoing cycle of discrimination against BIPOC students for generations.[5] Though this is not surprising, it is concerning, especially if we consider the dire effects such censorship will have on BIPOC students, just as it did for generations before them. Those of us who study and research Latinx/Chicanx literature, cultural studies, and culturally relevant pedagogy are familiar with the assimilationist strategies employed by the U.S. education system. We are also familiar with the deficit model of education, which sought to characterize cultural knowledge such as being bilingual or coming from a working-class family as a deficit.[6] What this censorship of books represents is a return to the deficit model of education and more through the desire to erase, negate, and make invisible the lives, experiences, and voices of BIPOC. In the case of book censorship in Texas, of particular concern is the effects that this will have on Latinx and Chicanx students and

---

4. I originally wrote this manuscript as my dissertation in the year 2011. It was common to use the terms *Chicana* and *Latina* at the time. However, since then, the terms *Chicanx* and *Latinx* have become labels accepted as being more inclusive of gender identity alongside ethnic identity. In an effort toward inclusivity and with the knowledge that many people beyond academia and activist circles find these terms divisive, I've chosen to use *Chicanx* and *Latinx* when discussing multiple genders, *Chicana* and *Latina* when discussing women and girls specifically, and *Chicano* and *Latino* when discussing men and boys.

5. For the purposes of this research I will be examining the US education system. In using the term *US education system* I am referring to the use of Anglocentric and assimilationist pedagogies that ignore, silence, or negate the cultural practices of BIPOC. However, I acknowledge that other global systems of education may also be marked by discriminatory pedagogies and practices.

6. Angela Valenzuela discusses the deficit model of teaching and, alongside other scholars, negates this concept by now insisting on characterizing the cultural knowledge students come to the classroom with as an asset. She discusses these notions at length in her text *Subtractive Schooling: U.S.-Mexican Youth and the Politics of Caring*.

their futures. I argue that this censorship is another form of assimilationist pedagogy.[7]

METHODOLOGY AND MY ACADEMIC *TESTIMONIO*

Using interviews, analysis of *testimonios* (testimonies) and literature, Chicana feminist theories, and culturally relevant pedagogies, this book will address the effects of assimilationist and Anglocentric schooling on Latina and Chicana students' identities and connections to their cultures. This book highlights the education/educación conflict many Latinas/Chicanas encounter when entering the U.S. education system (K–12).[8] Through analysis of history, literature, pedagogy, and testimonios, I demonstrate that Latina/Chicana students often feel disconnected from their cultural identities once thrust into the Anglocentric school system, forcing them to experience this conflict in identity. It is fundamental that educators recognize and become aware of this conflict of identity so that we might rectify this issue. I argue that part of the solution to this conflict lies in what I call a *mestizaje* of epistemologies.[9] A mestizaje of epistemologies seeks to reenvision and reimagine the term *mestizaje*, utilized by Gloria E. Anzaldúa in her seminal text *Borderlands / La Frontera: The New Mestiza*. I call to mind the origins of the term *mestizaje*, which refers to a blending of cultures, while also extending this term and using it to describe epistemologies and pedagogies of the home and school. Specifically, I argue that a mestizaje of epistemologies occurs in the third space of education, much like Homi Bhabha's third space and Anzaldúa's concept of *nepantla* (the

---

7. I define this term as one that uses Anglocentric pedagogies as the norm and thereby the standard by which all students are measured, which becomes problematic for Latinx/Chicanx students who wish to maintain their cultural ties. I use *Anglocentric* to refer to the cultures and ideologies of Anglos, or Americans of English descent.

8. I distinguish between the terms *education* (meaning the knowledge acquired in the K–12 U.S. education system) versus *educación* (the knowledge acquired in the Latinx/Chicanx cultural/home environment).

9. I utilize this concept in my discussion of Native American identity and education in the article entitled "A Mestizaje of Epistemologies in *American Indian Stories* and *Ceremony*." I will elaborate on this theory further in chapter 2.

in-between space).[10] In this third space, an individual—or, for this discussion, a Latina/Chicana immersed in the U.S. education system—may encounter what I call the education/educación conflict, where one's epistemology directly conflicts with Anglocentric epistemologies and pedagogies.[11] Further, students who experience this conflict may shift into the third space of education if they become aware of it through conscious reflection, much like Anzaldúa's path of *conocimiento* (consciousness).[12] In an attempt to reclaim their identity through this conscious reflection, individuals may attempt to retain ties to their culture while at the same time attempting to bring home some of the knowledge acquired from school that had previously not been known by preceding generations. For example, in my multiethnic literature classes, I expose my students to the historical and cultural context surrounding specific texts such as Américo Paredes's *George Washington Gómez* and Jovita González and Eve Raleigh's *Caballero: A Historical Novel*. In the case of each text, I begin our discussions by providing historical context about events such as the Mexican-American War and the Treaty of Guadalupe Hidalgo or the violence that occurred on the United States–Mexico border between 1900 and 1915 and the violence enacted against Mexicans by the Texas Rangers. Students often react with shock and disbelief that they never learned about such historical narratives, and they usually take the time to share this knowledge with their families; in some cases, students will offer their texts to their families and friends to read for themselves. In response, many students' families will relay their own family stories relating to such historical periods, thus helping to reestablish these connections to their cultural identities, communities, and families. I argue that the difference in utilizing the term *mestizaje* as it is used

---

10. I will elaborate and problematize the term *mestizaje* in more detail within the following chapters.

11. I utilize the term *epistemology* to refer the "'system of knowing' that is linked to worldviews based on the conditions under which people live and learn" (Bernal 106). When referring to the cultural epistemologies of Latinxs, I refer specifically to a system of knowing that has developed because of the experiences within individuals' home and cultural communities. I utilize institutional epistemologies to explain Anglocentric ways of knowing that claim Anglocentric knowledge is the universal norm and standard by which everyone, especially students, should abide to succeed academically.

12. I will define and further discuss the concept of conocimiento in my next chapters.

here lies in blending home/cultural knowledge with school epistemologies in both spaces using conocimiento and understanding their education/educación conflict.

This book further examines how Latina/Chicana students may become aware of their education/educación conflict as they are immersed in challenging circumstances and encounter discriminatory pedagogies and epistemologies. One tool I employ to analyze discriminatory experiences in K–12 and higher education is testimonio.[13] I will examine the written education testimonios of Latinas in higher education via the Latina Feminist Group's *Telling to Live* text. I will also investigate the testimonios of my students about their schooling experiences in K–12 and higher education. Before reviewing their testimonios, I share my educational experiences and what brought me to this work.

My experiences in K–12 were uneventful ones; I cannot say with certainty that I ever experienced discrimination and racism based on my identification as a Mexican American student, though it is entirely possible that I encountered more covert forms of systemic racism. I attended private schools from kindergarten through twelfth grade in San Antonio, Texas, a predominantly Hispanic city. Most of my classmates were Hispanic, though my teachers' backgrounds varied and the class demographics diversified as I moved into high school. Reflecting on my experiences in K–12, I was not singled out because I was Mexican American. Still, I am white-passing, and most of my classmates were also Mexican American. At the same time, as I progressed in my schooling, I became acutely aware of the historical narratives and literature I was exposed to. As a San Antonio, Texas, student, I was subjected to many field trips to the Alamo and to the dreaded seventh-grade project in which we had to build a replica of the Alamo and offer a presentation on its importance in history class.

Seventh-grade Texas history is a rite of passage for students in Texas; it is a time when we are taught about the Mexican-American War, the "villainous" Santa Anna, and the victorious, heroic "defenders of the Alamo." This idea of Mexicans as the "bad guys" and the Alamo "defenders" as "good guys" is so ingrained in seventh-grade education that children like me found ourselves

---

13. For now I utilize the term *testimonio* to refer to the idea of testimony, but I will elaborate further on the context and history of this term in future chapters.

reenacting the Battle of the Alamo with chants of "Remember the Alamo" as we ran around the playground. While I unknowingly participated in these false narratives of the Alamo, I distinctly recall thinking that I would always be on the "winning" side because I was both Mexican and American. So, it seems some of me recognized the conflicting narratives that continue to permeate seventh-grade Texas history. I did not realize the irony involved in our seventh-grade Alamo project until many years later, when I discussed the problematic, propaganda-like narrative that positions Alamo fighters such as Davy Crockett and Stephen F. Austin as the heroes of the battle and the Mexicans as the villains. As with these history lessons, I also did not entirely understand that the literature we were exposed to often did not fully represent my culture and identity—hence my enthusiasm once I discovered Sandra Cisneros's *The House on Mango Street*, thanks to my aunt. Despite these pedagogical problems, I did not fully understand how problematic my education was until I, like my students, was exposed to literature, history, and cultural studies focused on Latinxs/Chicanxs during my doctoral studies.

I often share the story of why I chose this line of work and the texts I teach with my classes and at conferences, including my first reading of Gloria E. Anzaldúa's *Borderlands*. I was exposed to this text when I began my doctoral studies. I had never heard of Anzaldúa, even though my mother's family was from Brownsville, Texas—the Valley, as we call it—which was near Anzaldúa's hometown. I was shocked that someone could write in the style she utilized, and more importantly, I learned so much history about Mexican Americans from her book. It angered me that I had never been exposed to these historical narratives and this literature until I began my doctoral studies. As someone who always has students in mind because my initial intention when I graduated from college was to teach high school literature, I noted that if it had taken me this long to be exposed to Gloria E. Anzaldúa, Américo Paredes, Jovita González, and others, then that meant that most students would never learn about their histories and cultures if they did not reach higher education. I began to realize that the narratives that were presented in K–12 often ignored or silenced Latinxs/Chicanxs or positioned them as insignificant or invisible, thereby suggesting that Mexican American students and other BIPOC may have nothing to offer. Such assimilationist strategies were ones that I took note of in literature, testimonios, and the history of education.

EXAMINING THE EDUCATION/EDUCACIÓN CONFLICT

When I began my journey in academia, I sought to examine the effects of a discriminatory education system on Latina and Chicana students in K–12 and higher education (university or community college). More importantly, as I engaged in literary analysis of texts such as *George Washington Gómez*, by Américo Paredes, *Borderlands*, by Gloria E. Anzaldúa, and *Golondrina, Why Did You Leave Me?*, by Barbara Renaud González, I noticed that many of the characters within these novels represented various points in U.S. history in which Mexican Americans, Chicanxs, and Latinxs encountered conflicts of identity once they were thrust into a K–12 U.S. education system that predominantly utilized assimilationist strategies to teach students. As I continued my studies as a doctoral student and researched more examples of education discrimination from history, including cases such as *Mendez v. Westminster* (1946), the *Lemon Grove* case (1931), and countless other incidents, I realized that those students who survived and thrived in the U.S. education system did so because of strategies they developed or learned and that the key to those approaches often, though not always, lay with their home/cultural communities. I looked at Gloria E. Anzaldúa and Cherríe Moraga's "theory in the flesh" alongside my family's survival stories to better understand these strategies.[14]

When I first learned about Anzaldúa and Moraga's "theory in the flesh," I recognized something familiar. Before Anzaldúa and Moraga penned their theory, my great-grandmother Mama Nita and my grandma Esther practiced it through storytelling and wisdom sharing with their children and grandchildren so they would know where we come from and how they might navigate an Anglocentric world. Both women found it necessary to pass on their wisdom to the younger generations because they understood that schools would not.

Years later, when I began my doctoral studies with hesitancy and a reluctance to learn the daunting and unfamiliar terminology and methods of academia, I was drawn to the theories of Anzaldúa, Moraga, and other Chicana third space feminists because they drew on experiences similar to those of my

---

14. Moraga and Anzaldúa explain, "A theory in the flesh means one where the physical realities of our lives—our skin color, the land or concrete we grew up on, our sexual longings—all fuse to create a politic born out of necessity. Here, we attempt to bridge the contradictions in our experience" ("Entering" 21).

family. I must admit that academia made me uncomfortable and often forced me to question my intellectual abilities. I still feel that I do not quite belong and have much more to accomplish before I can think of myself as a confident scholar.[15] Though it has been years since my doctoral studies, I often confess to my students that I am still unsure of my place in academia and surprise myself with my knowledge and "expertise." Yet I was drawn to doctoral studies and coursework focusing on Latinx/Chicanx literary and cultural studies because they presented familiar stories about my culture and identity and provided current information with which I was unfamiliar. I was introduced to folklore that included corridos such as "El Corrido de Gregorio Cortez"; the novels of Chicanas and Latinas, such as Barbara Renaud González's *Golondrina, Why Did You Leave Me?* and Loida Maritza Pérez's *Geographies of Home*; and the work of Chicana third space feminists, such as Gloria Anzaldúa and Cherríe Moraga's *This Bridge Called My Back*.

As I continued along my academic path, it became apparent that I was not the only one who encountered this need to balance my cultural and academic selves. If I encountered specific texts, histories, and literature only because I decided to enter a PhD program, what about all the other Latinx students who do not make it as far in college or graduate school? This question, which I often pose to my students, has guided my work in helping to establish Mexican American studies in K–12 schools in San Antonio, Texas, and at my current institution, St. Mary's University, which identifies as a Hispanic-serving institution (HSI). In recent years, I have worked with the group Somos MAS to help in their efforts to expand Mexican American studies in K–12 classrooms in San Antonio and beyond. Somos MAS is responsible for the Texas State Board of Education's passage of an elective Mexican American studies course implemented and supported in high school curricula in Texas. With these efforts in mind, my advocacy outside the classroom became just as important as that in the school.

As a Chicana scholar, I became aware that I would need to work hard to maintain my identity while engaged as an academic scholar, which led to another question: How do Chicanxs/Latinxs maintain their cultural and

---

15. This uncertainty is felt by many women of color in academia. Such notions are referred to as "impostor syndrome," which includes "additional external questioning [that] isolates, demoralizes, and sets Latina/o students apart" (Hurtado and Sinha 174).

academic identities and epistemologies while "successfully" navigating an Anglocentric school system and academic environment? Though it is difficult to maintain ties to my cultural identity, I often place it at the forefront of my academic life and work, as evidenced by my work as the chair of the Hispanic Heritage Month committee and the implementation of multiple interdisciplinary events, including lectures by the Texas state poet laureate at the time, Lupe Mendez; screenings of the movie *Selena*; and student-led panel discussions addressing the importance of Anzaldúa's *Borderlands* text and theories. As the lone Chicana in my English department for several years, I leaned into my Mexican American studies research, background, and identity, refusing to back down in cases when I knew that we as a university or department needed to focus on how we might better serve our Latinx and first-generation students at St. Mary's University. I discovered ways to maintain my identity and insisted that my epistemologies and identity were legitimate academic areas of scholarship. Though I have the opportunity as a professor and academic to bring issues to light such as legitimizing Mexican American and ethnic studies in academia and offering opportunities such as validation of students' cultural backgrounds and knowledge, I recognize that some of my students do not feel that they have these opportunities and find themselves in complicated situations where the privilege of being able to contemplate one's identity in society, let alone advocate for their culture and community, might not be an option.

My experience has helped me succinctly define one of the problems many Latinas/Chicanas encounter. If we are all immersed in an education system, whether that is K–12 or higher education (university and community college), that privileges education, which is marked by Anglocentric pedagogies and ways of knowing, over educación, how does it affect Latinas' and Chicanas' success or failure in school, their relationships to their families, and their identities? However, exploring the history of Latina/Chicana education, literature, and testimonios demonstrates that Latinas/Chicanas encounter the education/educación conflict.[16] Once introduced to the U.S. school system, Lati-

---

16. I will define and thoroughly explore this concept in detail in chapter 2. Throughout this manuscript I will reference scholars who have examined the differences between education and educación. Of particular importance is that the research on this topic continues in various disciplines. Especially important is Carmen Guzman-Martinez's *Chicana and Chicano "Pedagogies of the Home": Learning from Students' Lived Experiences*, in which she explores how the pedagogies of the home aid students in their formal education and vice versa.

nas/Chicanas begin to privilege education—the Anglocentric, assimilationist epistemologies—over educación, which includes the *consejos* (advice), *cuentos* (stories), and knowledge of their home and cultural community. This privileging instills a sense of alienation from family and community while also creating identity confusion for Latinas/Chicanas. The combination of alienation, shame, and confusion may interfere with a Latina/Chicana student's ability to navigate her way through K–12 and beyond successfully. A Latina/Chicana may then choose to reject the epistemologies of school for her cultural knowledge or vice versa, leading to even more complex identity problems; this becomes even more pronounced for women of color within academia. I also encountered this subtle distancing from my family and culture as I became engrossed in my studies, though a new balance has emerged in recent years.

I argue that part of the answer to the dilemma many Latinas/Chicanas face emerged in my struggle. I realized my relationship with my family and cultural community was the answer. I realized I could maintain multiple identities and weave cultural and institutional ideologies together. Remembering that I once maintained this delicate balance was all I needed. This idea of weaving multiple epistemologies had been part of my life long before I knew I would need it to resolve my identity conflict. Our family's tradition of storytelling, emphasizing the use of Spanish at home, and maintaining connections to our culture continuously reminds me that I am not only a scholar but also a Chicana one. From my grandmothers, my mother, and all the women in my family, I learned the importance of weaving education and the educación of our home together.

To understand how problematic this education/educación conflict is, I explore its effects via Latina/Chicana education, literature, pedagogy, and testimonios. Critical race theory (CRT), a theory used by scholars such as Dolores Delgado Bernal to explore home/school epistemologies and engage in a critical analysis of the effects that the current U.S. education system has on Latinas'/Chicanas' identity, relationships to families, cultural communities, and success in school, is a valuable tool to use in examining this conflict. Specifically, I explore how a Latina or Chicana may often become confused regarding her identity; for example, there may be instances of discrimination or assimilation that ask her to reject her cultural identity or risk failure and rejection while experiencing alienation from family and cultural communities.

Despite the difficulties that some Latinas/Chicanas experience, I will demonstrate how they develop specific survival strategies, such as a mestizaje of epistemologies, a balancing of cultural and institutional knowledge employed through particular methods such as *la facultad* (the power of the mind and body to sense danger) and coming into consciousness via the path of conocimiento, differential consciousness, and the decolonial imaginary.[17] Such skills encourage acceptance of a Latina's/Chicana's self-identity while strengthening bonds with family and cultural communities and empowering them to succeed in academia. The adoption of a mestizaje of epistemologies is manifested via activities such as sharing family stories, retaining native languages, critical reflection on achieving awareness of one's positionality in the education system and society, and learning about one's cultural traditions at home in addition to those at school that tend to reflect the hegemonic cultural ethos of the nation. I will begin my analysis by examining Latinas/Chicanas in K–12 and beyond with their encounter with the education/educación conflict and their attempt to overcome it via adopting a mestizaje of epistemologies. I will continue my examination via the various methods Latinas/Chicanas develop to balance multiple epistemologies as portrayed by Latina/Chicana protagonists and writers in Latinx/Chicanx literature.

This study may allow me to demonstrate how detrimental the current U.S. education system is to some Latina/Chicana students, emphasizing the significance of establishing Mexican American studies programs in K–12 classrooms and beyond. Especially problematic are the effects that the education/educación conflict has on the academic success of Latina/Chicana students, their relationships with families and communities, and the acceptance/denial of their identities. The current U.S. school system insists that Latina/Chicana students choose Anglocentric epistemologies, via assimilation, over their cultural knowledge, thereby demanding that they also reject their cultural identities in favor of of assimilated versions of themselves (Castellanos and Gloria 81).[18] Such dualistic ways of thinking are problematic because they instill confusion about identity and, in some cases, cause students to reject their identities completely in favor of assimilation, as we see in texts such as *George Washington Gómez* and many others. Latina/Chicana students who find themselves conflicted by such cultural identity conflicts cannot succeed in

---

17. I will discuss each of these theories in more detail in the following chapters.

18. Multiple scholars throughout the years have identified this problem in the U.S. education system, including Laura Rendón in her text *Sentipensante*, Gloria Anzaldúa in *Borderlands*, Emma Pérez, and Chela Sandoval, among others.

institutions that encourage such thinking. It thus becomes necessary to begin "healing the split," as scholar Gloria Anzaldúa indicates in her discussion of dualistic ways of thinking, which starts in the U.S. education system (*Borderlands* 102).

CHAPTER SUMMARIES

I begin my analysis in chapter 1 by briefly examining the education/educación conflict as it is revealed throughout history. While my analysis of the history of Latinx education is brief, I specifically focus on definite points in Latinx education to set up my discussion of the current issues surrounding Latina/Chicana education today. My analysis of the history of Latinx education begins with the European conquest and the separation between Indigenous and Latinx identities and epistemologies. I continue exploring Latinx education in the mid-nineteenth century, pointing out the divisions that occurred because of class and sex. I examine El Movimiento, or the Chicano movement, and the various changes that happened despite systemic obstacles, such as the implementation of ethnic studies programs for Latinxs and Chicanxs during the mid-twentieth century, to demonstrate the attempt on the part of the movement and Chicanxs to include more diverse and inclusive pedagogies that represented their cultures. The movement included the walkouts of hundreds of Chicanx students in protest of the racist pedagogies and conditions of their schools in California, Texas, the Southwest, and elsewhere. While El Movimiento did achieve many education reforms, in the decades that followed, other great changes also occurred. Nevertheless, problems persisted, such as the passage of California Proposition 209.[19] In the years since I began this project, other problematic issues have permeated the already dire

---

19. "California Proposition 209, the Affirmative Action Initiative," was on the ballot in California as an initiated constitutional amendment on November 5, 1996. Proposition 209 was approved.

"A 'yes' vote supported adding Section 31 to the California Constitution's Declaration of Rights, which said that the state cannot discriminate against or grant preferential treatment based on race, sex, color, ethnicity, or national origin in the operation of public employment, public education, and public contracting" ("California").

education system, including the banning and censorship of books by and about LGBTQIA+ individuals and people of color, laws making it unlawful to teach CRT in K–12 classrooms (though this concept has never been taught in K–12), and limitations placed on teachers in addressing issues such as systemic racism, discrimination, and certain historical events focused on issues of race and gender.[20] I continue discussing Latinx education by analyzing the present-day dilemmas Latinxs face because of laws enacted in the early 2000s in states such as Alabama, Arizona, and Mississippi and the current laws regarding CRT and book censorship in Texas, Florida, and Oklahoma.

Chapter 2 allows me to transition from discussing the history of Latinx education to identifying the education/educación conflict encountered by Latinxs. I define the education/educación identity conflict as the inability to balance formal education attained in school with the educación of the home, thereby leading to uncertainty about one's identity. To resolve this identity dilemma, I contend that Latinas/Chicanas must attain awareness of their position between multiple educational ideologies, allowing them to move into the third space of education, where Latinas can survive and thrive and where multiple educational ideologies coexist. In the third space of education, Latinas' formal education and educación are balanced once they begin to practice applying a mestizaje of epistemologies in their academic and cultural lives.

I utilize Chicana third space feminism and CRT to develop my theoretical approach, which deconstructs Latinas'/Chicanas' identities, their experiences within the U.S. education system, its effects on their multiple epistemologies, and the impact on their relationships with their families. This chapter relies on the theoretical underpinnings of various scholars and concepts: Gloria Anzaldúa's path of conocimiento and la facultad, Emma Pérez's decolonial imaginary, Chela Sandoval's differential consciousness, Paulo Freire's critique of the

---

20. The recent backlash against LGBTQIA+ individuals and people of color emerged in response to the election of Trump and similar-minded politicians who deemed discussions about race and gender "inappropriate" and discomforting to school-age students. In Texas in particular, teachers may not discuss CRT, though this concept is not one taught at the K–12 levels; rather, the law uses coded language meant to control what can and cannot be discussed or read in K–12 classrooms. Similar laws have been passed in Florida and Oklahoma, and there are policies being proposed that would also prohibit these same discussions at state universities in these states.

"banking" system, Michel Foucault's "figure of the ideal soldier," and Laura Rendón's *sentipensante* ("to think and feel," from the verbs *sentir*, "to feel," and *pensar*, "to think") pedagogy. I weave these ideas to develop my concept of a mestizaje of epistemologies. In the following chapter, I move from the concept to applying this theory to the literary analysis of texts by Latinas.

After theorizing about the education/educación conflict, in chapter 3, I will focus on the application of my theory of a mestizaje of epistemologies as lived by the protagonist of Barbara Renaud González's *Golondrina, Why Did You Leave Me?* I will demonstrate the significant impact formal schooling has on the identities and communal/familial ties of the protagonist in *Golondrina*. I contend that the protagonists of the text experience alienation from their families, cultures, and communities once exposed to U.S. school systems, which leads to the development of an education/educación conflict as they continue to work through the education sites, particularly K–12. I will reveal how the protagonists of *Golondrina, Why Did You Leave Me?*, Lucero and her mother, encounter a cultural identity conflict and resolve it once they know their positionality between multiple educational ideologies. Lucero's understanding of her unique position shifts her into the realm of the third space of education, where she learns how to balance education with educación through a mestizaje of epistemologies; that is, she survives by weaving elements of both.

Similarly, in chapter 4, I apply my theory of a mestizaje of epistemologies to the education testimonios of Latinas. I explore testimonios presented in *Telling to Live: Latina Feminist Testimonios*, *This Bridge Called My Back: Writings by Radical Women of Color*, and *This Bridge We Call Home: Radical Visions for Transformation*. I examine the strategies Latinas in K–12 and academia have developed to balance multiple ways of knowing. I discuss how these women build strategies and solutions that involve a mestizaje of epistemologies in the third space of education to overcome the education/educación conflict.

I examine testimonios in which Latinas/Chicanas become aware of an education/educación identity conflict. I further demonstrate the complexity of this struggle by focusing on excerpts in which Latinas discuss how they cope with multiple epistemologies and identities. I demonstrate how Latinas/Chicanas in academia have resisted complete assimilation by sharing their stories and maintaining ties to their cultural communities, languages, and histories. While the women of each anthology speak from within the academy, the tools they have acquired are used to find their voices, write themselves back into history, and attain positions where they can establish changes in their cultural and academic communities. Rather than embracing assimilation, these women fight against it by taking the *his* out of *history* to focus on the woman's perspective rather than looking to "the universalist narrative in which women's experience is negated" (Pérez, *Decolonial Imaginary* xiv).

Chapter 5 continues my analysis and discussion of the education/educación conflict to examine education testimonios of current Latina students from my Mexican American literature class. This chapter contains testimonios in which Latina and Chicana students discuss navigating higher education while retaining ties to their cultural epistemologies and communities via a mestizaje of epistemologies. I conclude my discussion by reflecting on my reasons for engaging in this project, given the current state of the public education system in the United States, especially in Texas. I also point to avenues for continuing such research, especially considering the recent education trends regarding Latinxs in Texas and the South. A focused analysis of each Latina/Chicana protagonist's, writer's, and student's encounters with the education/educación conflict and their subsequent adoption of a mestizaje of epistemologies in their literature and education is a necessary effort that makes these issues visible to students and teachers alike. I end with discussing the various methods I utilize in my classes, including interdisciplinary approaches focusing on literature, historical narratives, antiracist pedagogies, and community, to help students retain ties to their cultural epistemologies and communities while obtaining a higher education and working to become agents of change in our society.

1

CONTEXTUALIZING THE EDUCATION/ EDUCACIÓN CONFLICT WITHIN THE HISTORY OF LATINX EDUCATION

To assess the current state of education in the United States and its effects on Latinas and Chicanas, I begin my analysis by contextualizing the education/educación conflict within U.S. history. I begin my examination of the history of U.S. Latinx education with the European conquest of the Indigenous peoples and various tribes of North America, including the Aztecs, Mayans, and Incas, to demonstrate how assimilation began severing ties to Indigeneity and cultural epistemologies.[1] Once Europeans arrived in the Americas, they aimed

---

1. I use the term *Indigenous* to describe the native inhabitants of the Americas. It is also a term used by various tribal members of the Americas to describe the "descendants of the First Peoples of these lands [the Americas]" (Yellow Bird 11). "Historically, and even in contemporary times, Indigenous Peoples in the United States and Canada have not regarded themselves as one monolithic racial society. While Indigenous Peoples have, in the past and the present, found common ground in their experiences and dealings with European American colonizers, they have also often viewed one another as diverse peoples, distinguishable according to language, behavior, dress, geography, foods, technologies, creation stories, and numerous other characteristics. Indeed, how Indigenous Peoples came to understand themselves and what they wanted to be called had a lot to do with how each people defined themselves in their own language, which was most often contextualized through their unique experiences and histories. The idea of dividing people according to a single racial identity was the invention of Europeans,

to conquer and colonize its peoples.[2] To succeed, Europeans realized it was necessary to control Indigenous people physically as well as to control their ways of thinking. Within this context, education scholars Sofia Villenas and Donna Deyhle note, "For the process of imperialism and domination to be more effective, they required the domination of the mind, of the worldviews and ways of life of the people" (417). Such domination could not ultimately occur until assimilation and acculturation took place. Scholars Merril Silverstein and Xuan Chen note that most definitions of acculturation indicate "that the minority ethnic group will incrementally adopt the ways of the majority culture and irreversibly will become more and more like it" (189). Europeans immersed themselves in the task of destroying Indigenous cultures while forcing their own cultural ideologies onto those who survived. For Europeans to accomplish the task of cultural genocide, the eradication of Indigenous peoples' knowledge and culture had to occur. The thrust toward assimilation thus began with the

> burning of Mayan, Aztec, and Incan libraries and books. Languages were repressed, and systematic attempts to destroy and eradicate whole cultures were colonial and then nation-state governmental policies. Schools in the United States effectively performed this task of instilling a hegemonic worldview. Indian boarding schools, for example, and the segregated Mexican schools of the Southwest had as their agenda the replacement of indigenous culture and beliefs with hegemonic European American worldviews that justified the practice of domination as the natural order of things. (Villenas and Deyhle 418)[3]

The burning of books and eradication of any ties to Indigenous epistemologies ensured that a separation occurred between those deemed Indigenous and

---

who socially constructed race to exclude and subordinate peoples who were not white and to privilege those who were" (Yellow Bird 1).

2. I utilize the term *Americas* to refer to the continent including North and South America and *America* to refer to the United States of America.

3. This method of colonization is particularly striking because it is one that persists today especially in states such as Texas and Florida, where attempts to control education via book censorship and banning have become a hot topic in recent years. The need to decolonize and push back against such methods is thus highly relevant.

those deemed Mexican. Once such ties were eliminated, Mexican and Indigenous peoples were further divided by the type of "education" systems they were forced into. This divide-and-conquer strategy ensured the eradication of ties between Mexicans and their Indigenous identities.[4] It continues to be used in the U.S. school system to further divide and conquer Latinxs on an individual and cultural level, thereby leaving them in a vulnerable position to be manipulated through assimilationist pedagogies and methods.

THE "BEGINNINGS" OF LATINX EDUCATION IN HISTORY AND HISTORICAL FICTION

Assimilationist strategies began with subjecting Latinxs to segregation, assimilation, and acculturation, although they could attend schools that were primarily dominated by Anglo students, a right denied to Native American students.[5] An especially significant point where we can locate a beginning discussion of Chicanx education is 1848, after the Mexican-American War and the establishment of the geopolitical border. At that time, many Mexican citizens were deterritorialized as they were suddenly stripped of their Mexican citizenship only to realize that they were American citizens; they were therefore unable to

---

4. The concept of dividing and conquering refers to military strategies employed by various conquering empires, including those of the European colonizers. Especially significant is the fact that this tactic was used by the Spaniards, including Hernán Cortés: "Spaniards either invited Indian allies to fight alongside them or fomented internal discord among tribes so that Indians fought Indians and Spaniards shed less blood" (Weber 146). This was a strategy that continued to be used by colonizing countries to instigate division among those they wished to colonize. I use this term to point out that division among Latinxs continues to be perpetuated by the Anglo hegemony, thereby allowing Anglos to maintain control of society and institutions such as schools.

5. There are numerous texts and extensive research available on Native American boarding schools. These texts include but are not limited to the following: Brenda J. Child's *Boarding School Seasons: American Indian Families, 1900–1940*; Jon Allan Reyhner's *American Indian Education: A History*; *Away from Home: American Indian Boarding School Experiences, 1879–2000*, by Margaret Archuleta, Brenda J. Child, and K. Tsianina Lomawaima; and Andrea Smith's *Conquest: Sexual Violence and American Indian Genocide*, among others.

discern to which country they belonged. Barred from claiming full citizenship in Mexico because of the Treaty of Guadalupe Hidalgo and prevented from enjoying the full rights of U.S. citizenship due to rampant racism, the Texas Mexicans and others along the newly created border found themselves cast into a new space between multiple worlds, cultures, and education epistemologies, borderlands of education.[6] This concept of the borderland of education is derived from Gloria E. Anzaldúa's definition of the United States–Mexico borderlands, which she describes as a "residue" of colonization, which she details as she describes the effects that the signing of the Treaty of Guadalupe Hidalgo had on Mexicans residing in Texas before 1848.

The Treaty of Guadalupe Hidalgo, signed on February 2, 1848, officially ended the Mexican-American War. The signing of the treaty guaranteed Mexican citizens certain rights that were unfortunately never honored. Specifically, the Treaty of Guadalupe Hidalgo guaranteed certain land and property rights as indicated in Article VIII: "Mexicans now established in territories previously belonging to Mexico and which remain for the future within the limits of the United States, as defined by the present treaty, shall be free to continue where they now reside or to remove at any time to the Mexican Republic, retaining the property which they possess in the said territories" (par. 18). In addition to property rights, personal rights regarding their culture, languages, and religion are also referenced in Article IX of the Treaty of Guadalupe Hidalgo: "The Mexicans who, in the territories aforesaid, shall not preserve the character of citizens of the Mexican Republic, conformably with what is stipulated in the preceding article, shall be incorporated into the Union of the United States and be admitted at the proper time (to be judged of by the Congress of the United States) to the enjoyment of all rights of citizens of United States, according to the principles of the Constitution" (par. 21).

Despite the promises made, the cultural identity dilemma faced by Mexican Americans was further complicated when racism interfered with the initial agreements of the treaty. While the treaty "guaranteed the linguistic, cultural and educational rights of the Mexican people who found themselves

---

6. I use this term to describe the in-between space of education for Latina/Chicana students, where the education received at school conflicts with the educación of the home. Scholars Gilberto Q. Conchas and Nancy Acevedo also use this term in their text *The Chicana/o/x Dream: Hope, Resistance, and Educational Success.*

in conquered territories," such stipulations were not upheld (Villenas and Deyhle 418). The treaty did not enforce the rights of Mexicans and instead implemented education programs that attempted to Americanize Mexican-origin students, thereby creating problems of identity for them (418). Instead, those Mexican people who were landholders often saw their land stolen from them by Anglos, schools segregated Mexican and Anglo children, and in some cases, the Spanish language was forbidden. Guadalupe San Miguel and Richard Valencia explain the effects that the treaty had on the education of the new Mexican American children: "local officials, such as city council and school board members, also established schools for Mexican-origin children in this post-1848 period, but since they were more interested in first providing White children with school facilities, the Mexican schools were few" (357). In response to this lack of schools, some Mexican communities banded together to establish schools for their children, known as *escuelitas*.[7] Eventually, the number of schools for Mexican children increased. However, these schools were often segregated yet retained the goal of Americanization or attempted to force Mexican students to adopt Anglo-American ideologies while remaining at the bottom of the socioeconomic ladder, which in turn often led to conflicts of identity for students who wished to retain their cultural ideologies.

The Jim Crow laws of the South served as the origins for the segregation of Latinx students from their Anglo peers and were often referred to as Juan Crow laws in the Southwest.[8] Much like the South's Jim Crow laws, Juan Crow laws in the Southwest focused on segregation by prohibiting interracial marriages and controlling the politics of the area in many ways. Monica Muñoz Martinez elaborates on the issue of Juan Crow laws in her exploration of anti-Mexican violence in Texas in her book *The Injustice Never Leaves You: Anti-Mexican Violence in Texas*. Martinez notes that Juan Crow laws "insisted on the new code of social relations, which in turn initiated a new racial hierarchy.

---

7. Much has been written on the history of escuelitas, including, most recently, Philis Barragán Goetz's *Reading, Writing, and Revolution: Escuelitas and the Emergence of Mexican American Identity in Texas*.

8. Roberto R. Treviño and other history/education scholars point out that the Jim Crow laws of the South affected not only African Americans but Mexican Americans as well. In some places, such as Texas, Mexicans experienced segregation more than permanently settled African Americans.

Political battles took shape over local governments. The newcomers [Anglo-Americans] moved to disenfranchise Mexican residents and minimize their social or economic influence ... According to Anglo settlers, ethnic Mexican residents did not merit the rights and privileges of Americans despite their status as legal citizens and their long history in the region" (16).

Interdisciplinary studies and historical novels such as Américo Paredes's *George Washington Gómez* help to highlight the segregation and racist practices employed by the U.S. school system. Paredes's text plays a pivotal role not only in literary studies but historically as well because it is one of the first "Chicano" texts to examine the effects that the Treaty of Guadalupe Hidalgo had on Mexico-Texans, those Mexicans who were already residing in Texas before the Mexican-American War and the signing of the treaty. The text, though a work of fiction, chronicles numerous historical instances in south Texas, including the war between *los sediciosos* (the seditionists) and the Texas Rangers, the influence of politicos at the time, and systemic racism embedded in the school system. For my purposes here, the fictional retelling of the segregation and racist practices of the U.S. education system in south Texas during the early 1900s plays a pivotal part in helping to understand the history of Mexican American education.

USING LITERATURE TO UNDERSTAND THE HISTORY OF CHICANX EDUCATION

Paredes's *George Washington Gómez*, written in the 1930s and published in 1990, serves as a bildungsroman and explores the education of the title character as he attempts to hold on to his culture throughout his school years. *George Washington Gómez* follows the exploits of Guálinto/George from the moment he is born. Of particular significance is his family's wish that he become a "leader of his people" when he grows up. This term implies that he will become "educated" by attending school and eventually use that education to help the Mexican American people and his community by becoming a lawyer or doctor. However, Guálinto soon discovers that his attempts to become a "leader" are met with racism every step of the way, especially with his first teacher, Miss Cornelia, a woman who is described as having darker skin that she covers up with layers of white face powder to emulate the white teachers and women in town. From the first day of school, Miss Cornelia exhibits a hatred toward Guálinto, perhaps due to his naivete, willingness to learn, and intellectual abilities. Miss Cornelia's disdain for Guálinto can also be read as a form of internal racism on her part. Still, he represents someone who desires a different outcome for himself despite his circumstances. Though Guálinto demonstrates signs of superior intellect, he must work within the confines of assimilationist pedagogies, which require him to learn English and American ideologies: "By the time Guálinto went to school he could read Spanish, he could do simple arithmetic, and he knew some English . . . He was used to speaking out and being heard, to being right about many things. In class he always knew the answers to questions, or thought he did, and always wanted to answer them. This made Miss Cornelia furious, to the point that when he raised his hand she was apt to say, 'Shut up and put that hand down'" (125). Despite Guálinto's thorough understanding of his schoolwork and a demonstration of his intellectual capabilities, he is met with racist hostility by his teacher. It is this exposure to racism that makes Guálinto aware of his state as a minority in the U.S. school system. This experience, though fictionalized, reveals the historical encounters many Mexican American students in south Texas experienced at this time. Despite setbacks caused by racism, Guálinto is initially proud of his cultural background and attempts to retain his Mexican American culture and identity.

Guálinto/George initially opposes history lessons that leave out the oppression of Mexicans and the theft of their lands by Anglo-Americans. Paredes reveals the conflict Guálinto experiences while arguing about a history lesson regarding the Alamo: "the Mexicotexan knows about the Alamo; he is reminded of it often enough. Texas history is a cross that he must bear. In the written tests, if he expects to pass the course, he must put down in writing what he violently misbelieves" (149). Guálinto's desire to point out the flaws in the American school system, especially in history, reveals an awareness of his societal role and a need to change that position. By pointing out such disparities in history, Guálinto uses the education the American school system has given him to counter the hegemonic history it teaches. However, Guálinto also experiences a sense of alienation in the classroom as his teacher discusses the Alamo as portrayed by school textbooks. His inability to counter the Alamo story with the Mexican version leaves him angry and unsure of his identity.[9]

---

9. It is important to note that the historical narratives contested by Guálinto in *George Washington Gómez* continue to be problems faced by students today in states such as Texas, Florida, and Oklahoma, among others.

As Guálinto progresses through his education, he becomes more aware of his position as a Mexican American in an Anglocentric school system and society. Once in high school, Guálinto finds himself torn between complete Americanization or retaining ties to his culture: "In school, Guálinto/George Washington was gently prodded toward complete Americanization. But the Mexican side of his being rebelled" (148). As he progresses to college, however, Guálinto concludes that he can succeed only by assimilating and succumbing to the world of hegemony or the dominance of Anglocentric norms and ideologies. As Cordelia Barrera notes in her discussion of Guálinto's identity conflict, he is a "would-be hero who ultimately disidentifies with his past, resulting in his continued fragmentation of self and identity" (101). His struggle between Americanization and maintaining his Mexican culture reveals an identity dilemma for many Mexican Americans and a question of how to balance multiple epistemologies. Guálinto is confronted with opposing binaries such as Mexican versus American, which positions Mexican identity as inferior to American identity. He therefore finds that to succeed in an American world, he too must privilege American identity over his Mexican one or risk failure.

Though Guálinto is inspired to rebel against the hegemony in high school, his college education and experiences away from the border seem to subdue his counterhegemonic ideas. Paredes reveals Guálinto's change in attitude: "You don't have a chance anyway ... you won't be able to get many Mexicans to vote for you. Oh, they'll come and eat your *carne asada* and drink your beer ... But in the end, it will be the same old story" (293). Not only Guálinto's rejection of his people and culture but also his refusal to help them demonstrate a complete reversal of his former attitudes toward Mexicans and Americans. Although he was once proud to be a Mexican, his alliance eventually rests with the Americans. Rather than identify his position as a proud Mexican American, Guálinto forgets, claiming his place in an Anglocentric world.

Guálinto's change in alliances seems to stem from the continuance of his American education. Guálinto learns who the powerful and the powerless are. This awareness encourages him to attain complete American assimilation to become part of the hegemony that oppresses and assimilates rather than attempting to use his new position to be a "leader of his people" (Paredes 40). Guálinto believes that Americanization, marrying an Anglo woman, rejecting his culture, working for the American government as a spy among his people, and ultimately forgetting his subaltern state and his minority status will afford him the powers and positions of Anglos.

At the same time, subconsciously, Guálinto still retains his rebellious nature. This is especially evident through his recurring dreams. In one such dream, Guálinto leads the Mexican army to victory against Houston and the Texans, allowing "Texas and the Southwest [to] remain forever Mexican" (Paredes 281). Not only does Guálinto imagine himself fighting a battle that has already been fought, but he also often wakes up "with a feeling of irritation" and wondering, "Why do I keep on fighting battles that were won and lost a long time ago?" (282). Rebellion remains part of Guálinto's subconscious despite his deliberate attempts at Americanization.

Other texts that explore the unique experience that Latinxs endured because of the Treaty of Guadalupe Hidalgo include Jovita González and Eve Raleigh's historical fiction text, *Caballero* (written in the 1930s and 1940s and published in 1996). Like *George Washington Gómez*, *Caballero* chronicles the impact that the Mexican-American War and the eventual signing of the Treaty of Guadalupe Hidalgo had on the Mexicans residing in Texas before the war. *Caballero* also situates its characters and the main conflicts within the context of historical events such as the usurpation of Mexican lands by Anglo-Americans, the intermarriage between Anglo-American men and Spanish Mexican women, and the ongoing violence that ensued. Of particular importance is the ideology that accompanies the physical takeover of Texas: assimilationist strategies encourage and, in some cases, force Spanish Mexicans to accept Anglocentric ideologies or risk losing everything. Because the text emphasizes these assimilationist tactics employed in society, we as readers begin to see the foundations of assimilationist schooling shortly thereafter. González and Raleigh's *Caballero* further reveals the dilemmas encountered by the protagonists during the imperialist colonization of Texas by the United States. González and Raleigh expose the women protagonists, Doña María, María de los Angeles (Angela), and Susanita, as new Mexican American citizens who must negotiate fresh societal roles. Like George/Guálinto, the women of *Caballero* are confronted with an identity conflict (though it is situated outside the school system) once Texas becomes part of the United States. The dilemma arises through exposure to education as interpellation and awareness of their positions between the former epistemologies of their cultural homes and the ways of knowing they must adopt once they forcefully become Americans. Such awareness propels the protagonists into a third space of education, which I define in detail in chapter 2, as they learn how to shift between multiple ways of knowing, establishing that they can no longer be part of the colonized, nor can they be part of the colonizers. In addition, these protagonists realize that they cannot fully embrace the epistemologies of the colonizer or colonized. Their identity conflict is further problematized because of their gender, resulting in additional strategies necessary to balance various epistemologies. Thus, like George/Guálinto, the women of *Caballero* are forced to decide between the epistemologies of their culture or that of the Anglos, or to integrate these into a new hybrid culture, a third space (Anzaldúa, *Borderlands* 100–101).

Though the women of *Caballero* do not encounter the education/educación conflict in the same way that Guálinto does, due to their status as women, they still are forced to choose between two seemingly oppositional epistemologies, that of the Anglo-Americans or that of their Mexican origins. Like Guálinto, the women of *Caballero* seemingly reject their oppressed status as double minorities because of their status as Spanish Mexican women living in a patriarchy-controlled society.

Because of the patriarchal power structure, the women of *Caballero* are forced to remain within the domestic sphere. Not only must they physically confine themselves, but they are also expected to be submissive, obedient, and silent possessions of the Mexican patriarchy. As submissive possessions, the women of *Caballero* represent the oppressed minority within their society. However, they retain a semblance of power, given their socioeconomic status in comparison to the Indigenous servants of their father. They become an oppressed people with limited access to cultural imperialism and the hegemony of the Mexican patriarchy. Despite the establishment of the Spanish Mexican patriarchy, Doña María, Angela, and Susanita, as oppressed figures, attempt to counter it, just as Guálinto initially attempts to. Susanita and Angela attempt to counter the hegemony by marrying Anglo men against their father's wishes. Rebellion against the Mexican patriarchy is evident, as "González depicts how such intermarriages often upset the patriarchal use of Spanish-Mexican women as objects of 'Spanishness' necessary to protect manhood and honor. As Don Santiago intensifies his confinement of his daughters to the private sphere in response to the Anglo-American invasion, his daughters Susanita and Maria de Los Angeles go against their father's wishes by leaving the confines of the private sphere and falling in love with Texas Rangers" (McMahon 242). By ignoring their father's wishes, Susanita and María break through the Spanish Mexican patriarchal traditions, which assert that daughters must be submissive. They also counter the idea that daughters are simply possessions passed on from father to husband.

Though González's portrayal of patriarchal opposition does occur in terms of the Spanish Mexican power structure, and while it seems that Susanita, Angela, and Doña María break free from the elitist Spanish power structure, they substitute one oppressor for another, namely the Spanish patriarchy for the Anglo. The problem arises because of the simplistic "solution" of ignoring their father's wishes, denying the old hegemony, and marrying into the new one. However, neither Susanita nor Angela can become full-fledged members of the new hegemony because of their former oppressed states. Awareness of her oppressed state does propel Susanita beyond it into a new kind of awareness in an in-between state where she can no longer embrace the epistemologies of her Spanish and Mexican cultures now that she has been exposed to Anglocentric ones. Susanita comprehends her role in society when Robert Warrener, her suitor, contemplates asking her father Don Santiago's consent to marry, realizing that "her father did not consider love important for marriage if other things outweighed it" (González and Raleigh 152). Susanita immediately dismisses speaking to her father because she realizes he controls her life and whom she marries.

Susanita's exposure to her oppressed state is further complicated when she is forced to choose between saving her brother and risking defying the laws of the Spanish hegemony. According to Spanish etiquette, women must remain within the domestic sphere unless accompanied by a male companion, usually a family member. Susanita's dilemma emerges as she contemplates her situation: "She would not . . . do it for Alvaro who had brought it upon himself, who so often had been mean to her, and was always selfish and exacting. But for mama, to keep her heart from breaking. For papa, longing for his son. And surely papa would love her again; he might even postpone the wedding in gratitude to her, and in time break it off" (González and Raleigh 262). Once again, Susanita realizes her oppressed state as she is forced to follow the laws of the patriarchy or risk becoming an outcast. Her decision to defy the laws of the Spanish hegemonic power structure allows Susanita to break free physically and mentally because of her new awareness.

Though Susanita has seemed to move beyond the realm of the Spanish hegemony, she is not able to completely disengage from the position of the oppressed since she chooses to marry an Anglo man. Susanita's decision to marry

Warrener is a substitution of the oppressive power of the Spanish patriarchy for that of the Anglo. Rather than being subjected to the Spanish patriarchy of her father, Susanita remains oppressed as a woman under the Anglo patriarchy. Her continued oppressed state is confirmed when Padre Pierre, the priest of her local church, announces, "Your duty lies with this man, and you must give him laughter and not tears; you must not weep for what has gone, not ever" (González and Raleigh 290). Susanita's marriage allows her to move beyond the old hegemony of the Spanish while also tying her to the new hegemony of the Anglos as both colonizer and colonized subject. Thus, Susanita's marriage propels her into a new position of awareness where she must find a way to balance some aspects of her former culture (Spanish) with that of her newly adopted culture, the Anglo-American. According to Frantz Fanon, Susanita's awareness and interpellation defines her as a native intellectual who cannot move beyond this state because "the native intellectual is not a true reactionary"; their method will not drive the colonizers away because they have adopted their way of life (21). As a native intellectual, Susanita can rebel against the Spanish patriarchy, but her position within the new Anglo patriarchy does not involve an actual act of rebellion. She does not fight against the colonizers; instead, she joins their forces to an extent, much like George/Guálinto does, choosing assimilation instead of finding a way to balance multiple epistemologies. Such decisions made by both protagonists reveal the lack of choices that Mexican men and especially women of the late 1800s and early 1900s faced when up against assimilation and acculturation at home, school, and society. One could argue that their decisions to assimilate were strategic ones meant to survive in a profoundly racist and sexist society.

Similarly, Susanita's sister, Angela, appears to have moved beyond the realm of the oppressed into hegemony. In reality, Angela has transcended into the oppressor position, where she remains simultaneously a part of and apart from the colonizer/colonized paradigm. Angela's move beyond this state occurs when she contemplates whether or not she has disobeyed her father, for "if she had disobeyed her father—this was something belonging to God, and God's things came first. She had done no wrong and had been properly chaperoned all of the time" (González and Raleigh 188). Once Angela is aware of her father's control over her life, especially regarding the man she marries, she can break free from her oppressed state within the Spanish patriarchy. However, Angela immediately dismisses any questioning of her decision because she believes it is God's will.

Though Angela's awareness of her state does move her beyond the oppressed realm, she does not fully break free from it. Instead, Angela substitutes one power structure for another. At the same time, Angela takes on a specific power of her own when she decides to speak against her father and decide regarding her own life, allowing her to transcend her subaltern status to the postsubaltern. When confronted by her father about her impending marriage, Angela explains, "I kept it all to myself because I knew it was a thing alone for me to decide, and mama would have considered it her duty to forbid me to think further or write to the senor" (González and Raleigh 311). She ultimately decides not only to marry but to decide what to do with her life rather than leave it to her father.

Despite Angela's opposition to her father, her awareness of her former state does not allow her to enter the hegemony powerfully. Instead, she becomes a subject of hegemony because she is required to assimilate the culture of the oppressor. Fanon suggests that "to assimilate the culture of the oppressor and venture into his fold, the colonized subject has had to pawn some of his own intellectual possessions . . . he has had to assimilate . . . the way the colonialist bourgeoisie thinks" (13). By thinking about her choice for marriage or merely engaging in conversations with an Anglo man, Angela begins to absorb some of the Anglo culture. Thus, her culture is pushed aside in favor of the oppressor's. Though awareness of her state has allowed Angela to move beyond the oppressed, her assimilation into the Anglo culture does not allow her to move into the hegemony. Angela is then subjected to the position where she is a part of the colonizer/colonized and, simultaneously, a member of neither. She reaches a point where she can no longer claim the original traditions of her people while also desiring to move forward by assimilating into the Anglo culture. Angela is then stuck between the worlds of colonizer and colonized because of a new awareness of her state.

Doña María also becomes aware of her oppressed state within the colonizer/colonized paradigm as she begins to question the patriarchal authority of her husband. When given the choice between peace and family unity versus violence and disturbance of the family unit, Doña María opts for peace despite its contradiction to culture and tradition. Her growing awareness of her subservient position within the patriarchal hegemony encourages Doña María to transcend it: "She had been too frightened to show resentment against his [Don Santiago's] domination in the early days of their marriage and had protected herself with the armor of meek submission. But the resentment had never died and now it came to give her strength" (González and Raleigh 85). Doña María admits that she was once an oppressed subject, unthinkingly obedient to her husband; she also questions her obedience and eventually stresses that she will no longer remain in this position.

Doña María's conscious awareness of her state allows transcendence beyond it, thereby allowing the attainment of limited powers, such as the ability to counter her former subservience. However, Doña María cannot gain full access to the hegemony and its power structure because she still retains a part of her subaltern self. She is still a woman within the Mexican patriarchal structure. She will also remain in the position of a Mexican woman within the Anglo patriarchal structure. Though she may gain some ground, Doña María transitions from the oppressed subject to the oppressor, in the process of which awareness and some powers are gained by questioning, thus countering the hegemony.

Works of literature such as *George Washington Gómez* and *Caballero* are essential elements of the history of Latinx education because they further demonstrate the education/educación conflict many Latinx students have encountered, while revealing the strategies they employed to work through such issues. Thus, analysis of these seminal "Chicanx" texts is a necessary element of understanding how the education system has impacted Latinx students. Though works such as *George Washington Gómez* and *Caballero* reveal how the Anglocentric content and attitude of education and epistemologies post–Treaty of Guadalupe Hidalgo led to questions of identity and cultural ideologies, the problem can also be attributed to the structure of the school system itself. As Michel Foucault discussed, this structure is based on the disciplinary techniques utilized in prison systems and the military. I will elaborate further on Foucault's discussion of the discipline of prisoners and its influence on approaches to them and soldiers' docile bodies as it concerns Latinx students in chapter 2.

LATINX EDUCATION IN THE MID-NINETEENTH CENTURY AND EL MOVIMIENTO

While some of the Latinxs of the post–Treaty of Guadalupe Hidalgo era struggled to adjust to assimilationist pedagogy and other racist structures of the school system meant to control them, the Latinx students of the mid-nineteenth century found ways to achieve higher education. Victoria-María

MacDonald and Teresa García's study of the history of Latinxs in higher education reveals that few people, regardless of race, gender, or ethnicity, obtained or participated in attaining a college degree during the mid-nineteenth century. Therefore, those Latinxs who were able to attend colleges were often from the "most privileged classes in the new territories as well as families from northern Mexico who sent their sons to receive a bilingual education" (MacDonald and García 20). The privilege of attending college and receiving a degree was reserved strictly for those Latinxs who could afford it (the upper classes) and restricted even further to only men. However, some women from privileged backgrounds were afforded this opportunity.[10] Up until recently, the focus on Latinos receiving a higher education far outweighed that on Latinas obtaining such schooling.[11]

The 1920s through 1950s saw an increase in the Latinx population attending colleges. Historians often refer to the adults of this era as the "Mexican American generation." This generation was the "first extensive bilingual, bicultural cohort of Mexican Americans in the United States" (MacDonald and García 24). This generation is especially significant because Latinxs from middle- and working-class families finally began entering college due to philanthropy and the GI Bill. MacDonald and García note that this generation's collegiate success deserves special attention because members often had to overcome formidable obstacles, including racism, discrimination, and harassment.

As a result of the racist attitudes of Anglos, Mexican American students were often "segregated into separate schools or classrooms based upon their accents, skin color or surname" (MacDonald and García 25). David Montejano indicates that Mexican American students were often segregated from their Anglo peers because of the perception of their "dirtiness," which was based on concepts of racial inferiority. Montejano notes that "the idea of

---

10. It is important to note that some Latinx students of working-class backgrounds were not even afforded the opportunity to finish out their elementary education, let alone higher education and college.

11. According to the 2010 census, the number of Latina students in college has surpassed the number of Latinos. The 2010 census and Pew Hispanic reports indicate that though the number of Latinxs in college has increased, the representation of Latinos continues to dwindle. Most recently, in the last ten years, we have seen a rise in Latinas attending and graduating from college, while the number of Latinos attending college has decreased significantly (Mora).

dirtiness was sufficiently ambiguous to accommodate the various interpretations of why the Mexican had to be kept separate" (228). In addition, "lack of enforcement of school attendance laws, language difficulties, immigrations, classroom harassment, and racism resulted in few Mexican American children even reaching eighth grade" (MacDonald and García 25). Between 1920 and 1950, the era saw meaningful educational changes for Latinxs. It was during this era that Latinxs struggled to gain access to the school system. Even though some Latinxs gained access to colleges at this time, this right went to a few privileged Latinxs. The 1950s signals the point at which middle-class Latinxs began to gain access to college due to GI bills and philanthropic efforts.

Once in U.S. school systems, Chicanxs and Latinxs discovered the need to alter the structures of the institutions of learning in both K–12 and higher education since the current structure demanded that Chicanxs and Latinxs eliminate the *"indio"* (Indian) part of themselves in favor of the part that was European via Spanish ancestry. El Movimiento, or the Chicano movement, sought to remedy the systemic racism and discrimination faced by students in K–12 and higher education. Historian Mario T. García explains what the movement entailed: "The Chicano Movement was the largest and most expansive civil rights and community empowerment social movement by people of Mexican descent up to the 1960s and 1970s. It was a reaction to the continued poverty and discrimination faced by Mexican Americans and lack of opportunities equal to those of other Americans" (4). Of particular significance during the movement was a focus on helping more Chicanxs and Latinxs obtain college degrees. Those Chicanxs and Latinxs who successfully climbed the academic ladder to become professors soon pushed a higher education agenda for their Chicanx and Latinx students.[12] Though

---

12. "In its search for Chicano history, the Chicano Movement spawned the first generation of professionally trained Chicano historians. The movement forced colleges and universities to expand and increase their enrollment of Chicano undergraduates and graduate students. A number entered into history programs and wrote dissertations on Chicano history. Because several acquired their PhDs in or around 1975, I refer to them as the Generation of 75 and more broadly as Chicano Movement–inspired historians. This includes myself, Richard Griswold del Castillo, Alberto Camarillo, Ignacio García, Ricardo Romo, Pedro Castillo, Arnoldo De León, and Gilbert G. González. Earlier pioneers of the Generation of 75 but also movement-inspired historians are Rodolfo Acuña, Mario T. García Juan Gómez-Quiñones, and Feliciano Rivera.

a small percentage of professors at the time were Chicanos and Latinos, and even fewer were Chicanas and Latinas, many Latinx students found it necessary to bring in more Chicanx and Latinx faculty. Carlos Muñoz points out that at the beginning of the *movimiento* (movement), "fewer than one hundred scholars of Mexican descent held doctorates in the US. Of these, most held doctorates in education (E.D.'s), which located them in a distinctly different research network with a very different emphasis from those scholars holding a Doctor of Philosophy" (Muñoz 141). MacDonald further notes that "the low number of faculty who might be interested in teaching or researching Latino issues was a principal issue addressed in the youth movement's conferences and lists of demands" (224). As part of the Chicano movement, young people organized youth movement conferences, including the 1969 Denver Youth Conference, where Mexican American youth gathered to discuss issues they faced, including systemic racism, discrimination, and injustice.

Of particular significance is the Chicano Coordinating Council on Higher Education, which organized the Santa Barbara conference of 1969, held at the University of California, Santa Barbara. At this conference, El Plan de Santa Barbara was developed and called for the "clearest and most detailed articulation of the demands of Latino college youth" (MacDonald and García 30). El Plan de Santa Barbara focused on three key areas: "[it] emphasized the obligation of college and university Chicanos to maintain ties with the barrio community. Second, it stressed the importance of changing institutions of higher education to open their accessibility to Chicanos. . . . Lastly, the Santa Barbara plan called for the alteration of traditional European White interpretations of history, literature, and culture to incorporate Third World viewpoints and particularly Chicano perspectives" (30). Many universities responded to these demands by implementing affirmative action policies to include more Latinx students and to admit more Latinx professors and administrators into the workplace.[13] Ethnic studies courses focusing on Chicanx literature, culture, and history were also added to curricula.

No Chicana historians received their PhDs at this time, but several would later, including Vicki Ruiz and Deena González" (García 14).

13. It should be noted that the affirmative action laws of the era mentioned in this chapter were eliminated by the Supreme Court in 2023.

Though significant changes occurred during this era, many Latinx and Chicanx students still struggle with identity. A vital dilemma addressed by Chicana scholar Gloria E. Anzaldúa in *Borderlands / La Frontera: The New Mestiza* includes her discussion of "linguistic terrorism" that emerges because of "Chicanas who grew up speaking Chicano Spanish having internalized the belief that we spoke poor Spanish" (80). Anzaldúa examines how Chicanx Spanish is often deemed an "illegitimate" "bastard language" (80). An introduction to school has often signaled and still signals the disappearance of Chicanx Spanish and Spanish language use. Especially significant is the rejection of Chicanx Spanish by Latinas and, along with it, the shame, the internalized belief that this language is not accepted. In the end, Anzaldúa points out that Chicanas end up oppressed by society when they converse in Spanish or Chicanx Spanish, thereby adopting the belief that they are wrong in maintaining home languages. Anzaldúa notes that "Chicanas feel uncomfortable talking in Spanish to Latinas, afraid of their censure" (80). In both cases, not only is there a rejection of the languages that Chicanas speak, but there is also a persecution of identity that is truly detrimental.

Such rejection and persecution reveal the inability of a Chicana to take pride in her identity. Anzaldúa asserts, "Until I am free to write bilingually and to switch codes without always having to translate, while I still have to speak English or Spanish when I would rather speak Spanglish, and as long as I have to accommodate the English speakers rather than having them accommodate me, my tongue will be illegitimate" (*Borderlands* 80). This example demonstrates how language further complicates the education/educación conflict, especially for Chicanas. The same can be said for Latinas who also engage with regional Spanglish, such as Tex-Mex, as Anzaldúa suggests. However, it is also important to note that some Chicanas' and Latinas' decisions to assimilate into English is often the result of exposure to linguistic terrorism, which causes them to reject their cultural language and even their identity. These oppressions, especially in terms of bilingualism, encourage many Chicanas and Latinxs to work toward transformations in education, especially in California, where the blowouts staged by Chicanx high school students progressed El Movimiento.

EL MOVIMIENTO AND THE CALIFORNIA BLOWOUTS

Like their collegiate peers, high school students and community members during the El Movimiento era became frustrated with the inequality of the education system. Though East Los Angeles community members called for reforms via channels such as legislators, school officials, hearings, and press conferences, no significant changes occurred. However, in 1963, a Mexican American Youth Leadership Conference was sponsored at Camp Hess Kramer, Malibu, California, for high school students. The conference was run by college counselors and teachers such as Sal Castro and Vickie Castro to encourage high school students to question their schools' racist pedagogies (Acuña 361). Many students who attended this conference eventually organized and participated in the blowouts of Los Angeles.

Shortly after the conference, Chicanx students found it necessary to call attention to the problems in their schools. That decision resulted in the blowouts or walkouts of March 1968, where "ten thousand students walked out of the mostly Chicano schools in East Los Angeles to protest the inferior quality of their education" (Bernal, "Grassroots Leadership" 113). Though Chicanos and Chicanas participated in the blowouts, much attention has focused on the leadership roles of Chicanos. In response to the lack of attention paid to Chicanas' role in the blowouts, Dolores Delgado Bernal interviewed several Chicanas who played vital roles in bringing about school reforms. Critical are the Chicanas' responses to the conference: "they remember the camp as a beautiful place where they were given a better framework to understand inequities and where they developed a sense of community and family responsibility. As one woman put it, 'these youth conferences were the first time that we began to develop a consciousness'" ("Grassroots Leadership" 118). Part of the development of that consciousness included the recognition that many of the problems Chicanx and Latinx students were having in school were linked to racism, sexism, and assimilation. Maylei Blackwell also discusses the development of Chicana consciousness, revealing that it was achieved through "familial bonds, female friendships, and relationships with political comrades" (61). The combination of campus and community identities, relationships, and epistemologies aided Chicanas in creating sites where they could resist the oppression they faced while also transforming society and the education system to their benefit.

Edward James Olmos's *Walkout* (2006), a movie depicting the blowouts, reveals how this consciousness came about. Especially poignant is a scene in which Paula Crisostomo, a real-life activist played by actress Alexa Vega, realizes that she hopes to have more opportunities than her parents did, as theirs were limited due to discrimination. Elyette Benjamin-Labarthe observes that Crisostomo's declaration is also her decision to refuse "a life of drudgery because of a lack of education, also at a deeper level, refusing the implicit laws of social reproduction, projecting her hopes on the chances of education as the sole means to improve her lot" (15). Crisostomo and other activists like her come to realize that their education system must improve so that their generation can move beyond the "drudgery" of their parents' lives while also holding on to their cultural ties.

Women such as Crisostomo played a vital role in protesting the inequality of their schools, especially by developing consciousness among community members. Activists attempted to raise consciousness through "informal dialogues with peers, family members or community members" (Bernal, "Grassroots Leadership" 127). Writing and other media were also utilized as weapons of consciousness-raising. Many women, such as Tanya Luna Mount, Crisostomo, and Celeste Baca, authored articles for activist newspapers such as *Inside Eastside* and *La Raza*. Essential are the writings of Enriqueta Vasquez in the newspaper *El Grito del Norte*.[14] Through such writings, these Chicana activities called attention to the oppressions they endured while encouraging Chicanxs and Latinxs to engage in transformational action. Of particular importance are Vasquez's writings from "The Woman of La Raza, Part I," reflecting on the comments expressed at the Denver Youth Conference in Colorado in 1969 in which the women declared, "It was the consensus of the group that the Chicana woman does not want to be liberated" (Oropeza and Espinoza 116). Vasquez responded, "The woman must help liberate the man and the man must look upon this liberation with the woman at his side, not behind, following, but alongside him leading. The family must come together" (121). Similar writings at the time called for a unification of the *"raza"* (race), calling on Chicanos to accept Chicanas as partners in the battle for equality.

EL MOVIMIENTO, LATINX EDUCATION, AND TEXAS

Shortly before the blowouts in California, Texas also experienced its movimiento calling for educational reforms. Much protesting for equality in the Rio Grande Valley schools emerged before the 1960s. Especially significant is

---

14. Enriqueta Vasquez's newspaper columns were published in the text *Enriqueta Vasquez and the Chicano Movement: Writings from* El Grito del Norte (2006).

the case of *Hernandez v. Driscoll CISD* (1957), in which a complaint was filed by Dr. Hector P. Garcia with the state superintendent of public instruction for the State of Texas in 1955. Scholar Enrique Alemán Jr. explores this case, in which his mother was a participating witness. The complaint described

> the institutionalized segregation practices employed by Driscoll CISD and its failure to meet the standard of the law as ruled under *Delgado vs. Bastrop Independent School District* (1948). In the Delgado case, the court ruled that school districts that arbitrarily segregated Mexican American students were doing so illegally and in a discriminatory manner; however, a school district was allowed to segregate first-grade Mexican American students if they were deemed to have English-language deficiencies. (6)

In the case of Driscoll, students with Spanish surnames were not evaluated for English proficiency and were instead placed in a "beginner's" first grade, then promoted to "low first grade" and "high first grade," thus spending a total of three years in first grade before moving on to second grade. The district's case eventually fell apart once students were called to testify, and many could do so only in English. This point in Rio Grande Valley history exemplifies the courageous acts of Chicanx students; such acts laid the foundation and are the precursors of what would later be known as El Movimiento.

Of particular importance in the Southwest was the "attention given to César Chávez and the farmworkers' movement, the politicization of Latinas/os/xs through Viva Kennedy clubs, and a growing desire to take advantage of federal War on Poverty programs and monies from private foundations contributed to the formation of student groups" (MacDonald 224). Farmworkers founded the Independent Workers Association in south Texas, the Rio Grande Valley, from 1966 to 1967, which eventually became the United Farm Workers Organizing Committee (Acuña 354). The groups formed included many Mexican American student organizations, such as the Mexican American Youth Organization at St. Mary's College, now St. Mary's University, and the University of Texas at Austin.

The Mexican American Youth Organization was founded by José Ángel Gutiérrez, Willie Velásquez, Mario Compean, Ignacio Pérez, and Juan Patlán, all college students at St. Mary's University. The organization's goal was to promote the idea of "la raza unida" (Montejano 59). On January 6, 1968, the first La Raza Unida conference, including 1,200 Southwest delegates, was held at Kennedy High School in San Antonio. With the assistance of the Mexican American Youth Organization, high school students began staging walkouts and boycotts to protest the lack of a better education (61). Such walkouts eventually encouraged similar actions in several south Texas towns, including Edcouch, Kingsville, Uvalde, Falfurrias, and Crystal City.

Other notable events affecting Latinx education in Texas included the protests that erupted because of discrimination in Crystal City High School. The Crystal City revolt of 1969 emerged in response to the Anglo teachers and alums reserving honors for their children while disregarding the achievements of Mexican American students. Marc Rodriguez notes that though Chicanx students represented many students in the Crystal City school system, they were denied certain rights and honors. Rodriguez explains how "glaring examples of this gerrymander of certain honors can be seen in the low level of Mexican American participation in the yearbook honors and some sports activities, such as the pompom squad where Anglo teachers and alumni controlled the decision-making process" (290). As a result of such blatant discrimination, students at Crystal City High School began to call for school reforms.

Unfortunately, those protests went unrecognized, and the students of Crystal City had no choice but to boycott the schools. The boycott eventually gained Chicanx students and their families the recognition they wanted. Federal mediators were brought in, and the school district agreed to consider "many of the student goals, including the establishment of bicultural and bilingual education, better testing of Chicanx student abilities and the election of student body positions and most titles by majority vote" (295). While the Crystal City boycotts did focus on the requests of Chicanxs, it is essential to note that problems of equal rights continued to persist for Chicanas and Latinas.

HISTORICAL SHIFTS FOR LATINAS IN SECONDARY AND HIGHER EDUCATION

Though El Movimiento established momentous changes for Latinxs in higher education, the focus continued to center on educating Latinos. Many Chicanos contributed to the suppression of Chicanas because of the "culturally accepted role of the woman which limits her to the house and church" (Saragoza 77). In addition, Chicanos held the belief that the "goal of the woman is to get married and to have children. Education is seldom emphasized. To have a high school diploma is a rarity" (77). In response to such sexism within their movement, Chicanas found it necessary to call for action. Once Chicanas began to call into question their role in the Chicanx movement, they realized that Chicanos refused to see beyond the prescribed roles that women were supposed to hold. Such division in ideology eventually led to a split between Chicanas and Chicanos.

The Chicano Youth Liberation Conference in Denver, Colorado, held in 1969 was one of the first conferences where the division within the Chicanx movement became quite evident. An examination of the origins of the Chicana movement reveals what occurred at this conference:

> A few vocal Chicana activists raised the issue of the traditional role of the Chicana in the Movement and how it limited her capabilities and her development. The majority of Chicanas participating in the workshop that discussed the role of the Chicana, however, did not feel the same. One Chicana observed that "when the time came for the workshop report to the full conference, the only thing that the representative did say was this—'It was the consensus of the group that the Chicana woman does not want to be liberated.'" (Saldívar-Hull 31)

In response to this conference, Chicanas began recognizing that awareness of their oppressive situation must be attained to engage in change. Such awareness resulted in founding Chicana groups on college campuses, sometimes with community-based organizations, such as the Mujeres Activas en Letras y Cambio Social and other organizations. As Chicanas became aware of the double oppression experienced while participating in the Chicanx student movement, they began to work toward educational reform, focusing on "Chicana classes, Chicana counselors, and Chicana teachers. It was felt that if Chicanas had the proper role models and classroom courses, eventual solutions to many of the socioeconomic problems confronting them could be found" (López 106). Though Chicanas and other Latinas began to fight for educational reforms and several changes started to take place, they continued to endure oppression. Chicana studies scholar Edén E. Torres writes about the conflict, "Some might think that by getting college degrees and an academic job I [as a Chicana] have achieved some measure of success. But what have I gained if I cannot talk to the person I once was? What have I earned if people like my grandfather automatically show me deference—when at the same time some students will disrespect me at every opportunity because I am a

Chicana?" (74). She aptly notes that those who managed to overcome racist, sexist, assimilationist school systems continued to be plagued with the problem of retaining contact with their cultural communities and establishing authority as Chicanas, both at home and in academic settings.

Gloria E. Anzaldúa also discusses the problems she encountered at school in Texas. She explains that there were no Anglos during her first school years because they were sent to another school. Anzaldúa notes, "all the teachers were white, and except for two or three, we got the dregs. All the best teachers were at Edinburg, teaching the white kids. We didn't have any music or art; we just had writing, reading, and arithmetic. But even the basics weren't taught that well" (*Interviews* 25). Anzaldúa explains that in her school career, she noticed the racism that occurred through the separation of the Mexican students from the Anglos and even the differences in how each group of students was taught.

The text ¡*Chicana Power!*, by Maylei Blackwell, further elaborates on women's involvement in El Movimiento, chronicling the emergence of Chicana feminism and many organizations formed by women to address issues of sexism within and outside of the Mexican culture. Chicana feminism, in particular, contributed to the discussion of various oppressions faced by women of color, now called intersectionality. Seminal Chicana feminist texts and literature at the time, including "La Feminista" by Anna Nieto-Gomez, sought to call attention to these multiple, intersecting oppressions while establishing a new idea of feminism that acknowledged various systems of oppression (Blackwell 208). These intersecting identities became especially important as Chicana feminism and other women of color feminisms emerged as part of the education dilemmas of the 1980s and beyond.

HISTORICAL PERSPECTIVES OF LATINX EDUCATION, 1970S-2000

Between 1970 and 1990, a significant increase in Latinxs pursuing secondary education occurred. MacDonald and García note that "from 1973 to 1994, the number of high school graduates enrolled in four-year institutions doubled, from 16 to 31 percent. However, college-bound Hispanics in four-year institutions only increased from 13 to 20 percent" (34). The low numbers of Latinx college-bound students caught the attention of the U.S. government for several reasons in 1980. Specifically, the government began to focus on educating Latinxs because the population of Latinxs increased significantly and very few were attaining college degrees. In response to the rising Latinx population, the U.S. government established several new amendments to improve retention rates, aid students financially, and train teachers to teach in locations dominated by Latinxs.

While the 1980s was dubbed the "decade of the Hispanic," it became apparent that Latinxs continued to experience problems in school. Though Latinx students had finally managed to gain access to school systems, the need to change such Anglocentric institutions to benefit Latinx students' success became apparent. MacDonald explains that in 1980, the government issued its first major report, *The Condition of Education for Hispanic Americans*, on Latinxs in schools. The report indicated that factors such as "high drop-out rates, low college participation, underrepresentation of Latinos in mathematics and science, and disparately lower scores on standardized tests than Anglo peers were among the items examined" that contributed to the failure rates of Latinxs in school (280). In response to such information, President Bill Clinton signed an executive order establishing an advisory committee that would oversee the "Educational Excellence for Hispanic Americans" (1990) meant to provide better opportunities for Hispanic Americans to "participate in and benefit from federal education programs" (282). The creation of the Hispanic Association of Colleges and Universities developed Hispanic-serving institutions (HSIs) to serve Latinx and low-income students.[15] Though the establishment of the Hispanic Association of Colleges and Universities and HSIs has certainly aided Hispanic students throughout the years, the question of whether these universities and colleges truly serve their Hispanic student populations continues to reign as a topic of discussion. Most notably, scholar Gina Ann Garcia's examination of "servingness" at HSIs reveals that enrollment percentage is often used to determine federal designation and therefore the moneys accompanying this designation; nothing more is offered in terms of support. Garcia argues that an "HSI organizational identity is more complex than a 25% enrollment threshold or federal designation. Both criteria are arbitrary, meaning neither the percentage of Latinx students nor the

---

15. HSIs are public or private two- and/or four-year not-for-profit degree-granting postsecondary institutions that enroll at least 25 percent full-time equivalent Latinx undergraduate students (G. Garcia 1).

federal designation defines what it means to be an HSI, or Latinx-serving" (1). Because of this lack of definition and criteria, the concept of the HSI often continues merely as a designation, though the number of HSIs steadily increases.[16] Garcia argues that we must redefine what it means to serve Hispanic and minoritized students and that there is a greater need to understand HSIs as "organizations striving to serve underserved populations" (3). Until new definitions of servingness are developed for HSIs, Latinx students will continue to face hurdles such as retention, belongingness, and graduation from institutions of higher education.[17] However, the 1980s signaled the beginning of great strides for Latinx education, though some problems persist, including the issue of sexism as experienced by Latinas and Chicanas.

LATINA-MESTIZA CONSCIOUSNESS, CHICANA THIRD SPACE FEMINISM, AND EDUCATION

The 1980s signaled profound changes in education and consciousness for Latinas, including scholarly work focused on the multiple oppressions experienced by women of color, their intersectionality, and how to address them. Those changes originated in the women of color feminist movement, which began in response to the U.S. white women's movement. Feminists such as Audre Lorde began to realize that the white women's movement was misunderstood entirely and did not represent women of color. In 1980 Lorde summarized the U.S. white women's movement in the essay "Age, Race, Class, and Sex: Women Redefining Difference" by explaining that "by and large within the women's movement today, white women focus upon their oppression as

---

16. According to Excelencia in Education, an organization dedicated to researching HSIs and Latinx college enrollment, retention, and increase in Latinx student college degree attainment, as of 2021–2022, there are 571 HSIs, and those numbers are increasing with emerging HSIs. See https://www.edexcelencia.org/.

17. As leading HSI scholar Gina Ann Garcia notes, current university structures and systems have been developed without Latinx students in mind, thus creating "white normative standards" that often interfere with the academic retention and graduation of Latinx students. Until we acknowledge these standards and contest them, Latinx students will continue to face systemic educational discrimination (3).

women and ignore differences of race, sexual preference, class, and age. There is a pretense to homogeneity of experience covered by the word 'sisterhood' that does not in fact exist" (375). In response to such feelings of exclusion and misrepresentation, women of color engaged in writings that challenged the white women's movement and their notions of feminism. Of particular importance are texts such as *All the Women Are White, All the Blacks Are Men, but Some of Us Are Brave* (1982) and *This Bridge Called My Back* (1981). Such texts allowed women of color to write as activists and voice resistance in the 1970s through 1980s in a social movement called U.S. Third World feminism. Sandoval argues that what U.S. Third World feminism "demanded was a new subjectivity, a political revision that denied any one ideology as the final answer, while instead positing a *tactical subjectivity* with the capacity to de- and recenter, given the forms of power to be moved" (*Methodology* 58). This "tactical subjectivity" emerges as a type of resistance, a survival strategy by women of color, which allowed them to weave between multiple ideologies.

Essential to this "new subjectivity" is the composition of the text *This Bridge Called My Back*. In the 1981 introduction, Cherríe Moraga and Gloria E. Anzaldúa explain that they hope the text will "radicalize others into action" (lvi). Furthermore, Moraga and Anzaldúa reveal,

> we envision the book being used as a *required* text in most women's studies courses. And we don't mean just "special" courses on Third World Women or Racism, but also courses dealing with sexual politics, feminist thought, and women's spirituality. Similarly, we want to see this book on the shelf of, and used in the classroom, by every ethnic studies teacher in this country, male and female alike. Off campus, we expect the book to function as a consciousness-raiser for white women meeting together or working alone on the issues of racism. And we want our colored sisters using this book as an educator and agitator around issues specific to our oppression as women. (lv–lvi)

Though *This Bridge Called My Back* did break ground in addressing the oppressions that women of color encountered in the 1980s, other anthologies that followed, including *This Bridge We Call Home*, admit that many of the same problems continue to exist.

This Bridge Called My Back is also a foundational text in Chicana third space feminism because of the imagery of the bridge, or *el puente*, that is evoked to demonstrate the need to bridge multiple worlds, cultures, and epistemologies.

Of particular importance is *This Bridge Called My Back*'s focus on writings by women of color and the discrimination they face due to their gender, sexual orientation, race, and class, as well as the intersections of all these oppressions. *This Bridge Called My Back* is one of the first texts by women of color addressing and calling out the oppressions they experience in society and institutions such as schools while also calling for reformations utilizing the concept of the bridge as a way to "bridge" or connect people of diverse backgrounds. Norma E. Cantú's exploration of Anzaldúa's use of the bridge image explains that it "forges not just a path, but creates a bridge, with all that that image connotes" ("Bridge" 11). The bridge imagery calls to mind the physical bridges between the borders of Texas and Mexico, such as those in Brownsville and Laredo. Referring to Anzaldúa and Moraga's use of the metaphor, Cantú explores the symbol of the bridge, asserting that "the bridge has been a physical connection, what has linked the two communities in Mexico and Texas. At the same time, the bridge is a symbol for the unity between the sister cities. The architectural structure spans the two nations, literally and metaphorically, the bridge, where we can safely place our hopes for the future. It is after all, the place for coming together, for healing ruptures" (11). These physical and spiritual bridges are needed to connect the multiple experiences and epistemologies of women of color. Critical is the "bridging" between the epistemologies of Latinas' formal learning institutions and their home cultures.

THE STRUGGLE CONTINUES AND BECOMES MORE COMPLEX

As MacDonald and García observe, the history of Latinx education in the United States demonstrates the transition between simply attaining access to the education system and, once there, realizing that access is not enough. In the first half of the twentieth century, Latinxs struggled to attain equal access to school systems that their Anglo peers attended. The second half of the twentieth century reveals that even though access has been attained, the Latinx education problem continues due to high dropout rates in high school, lack of retention at the college levels, and low test scores in high schools, in addition to other issues, such as bilingual and immigrant education.

Especially problematic is Latinx students' continued exposure to racism, sexism, and discrimination in the guise of Anglocentric curricula and pedagogy. Studies conducted on the cultural exclusion of Chicanxs in 1996 reveal that of three thousand students attending ten high schools in southern Arizona, "only 20 percent of the students in the study could identify two contributions that Hispanics had given the United States or the world" (Valencia 10). In short, the study concluded that "neither Mexican Americans nor students of other racial/ethnic groups had a good understanding of the history, culture, or contributions of the Mexican American people" (10).

Latinxs continue to feel a sense of not belonging to school cultures due to the lack of validation of their cultures. This sense of not belonging perpetuates a desire to belong to the Anglocentric hegemony of school and society, thereby instilling the inability to entirely belong to their cultural communities, as we will see in the coming chapters on testimonios from various generations and most notably from the education testimonios of Generation Z. Such examples are further provided in numerous works of contemporary Latinx literature, including Erika Sánchez's *I Am Not Your Perfect Mexican Daughter* and Julissa Arce's *You Sound Like a White Girl*. In both works, young Latina/Chicana protagonists are at odds between their cultural identities and Anglocentric society. In the case of *I Am Not Your Perfect Mexican Daughter*, the protagonist, Julia, finds herself at odds with her mother and family, especially after the death of her seemingly perfect older sister. The central conflict she encounters revolves around her consciousness journey, in which she begins to explore how her story is embedded within her own mother's as well. Though Julia is initially resistant to "traditional Chicanx notions of femininity by contrasting herself with her dead sister and mother," she eventually learns why her mother accepts such ideologies as she uncovers the stories of Amá (her mom), her sister, and eventually herself, thereby allowing for a balance of her cultural epistemologies and identity with Anglocentric ones (Cantú-Sánchez, "Fourth Choice" 9).

Julissa Arce's *You Sound Like a White Girl* also addresses the same identity conflict Julia experiences, revealing that this education/educación conflict remains problematic for Latinas/Chicanas. Arce's memoir-like text describes the various instances in which she is forced to assimilate to the Anglocentric society and institutions she finds herself immersed in. Though Arce points out that she seemingly does everything "right" to obtain the American dream, such as perfecting her "accentless" English, graduating from college, and obtaining a high-stakes job on Wall Street, she still feels this sense of not belonging. Eventually, she concludes that though she has been told that assimilation is the key to the American dream, one should reject it and embrace one's cultural identity.

While admittedly the 2010 census indicated a steady rise in graduation and retention rates for Latinxs, more so for Latinas since the 1990s, despite assimilationist pedagogies, unfortunately, the education of Latinxs has yet again come under fire. In the last few decades, the laws of Arizona, enacted because of the immigration debates currently dominating the country, have revealed that the fight to end discrimination in schools continues. In May 2010, Arizona governor Jan Brewer signed HB 2281, a bill banning ethnic studies classes that "promote resentment" of other racial groups. The new law does not allow the teaching of ethnic studies courses in K–12 that "promote the overthrow of the United States government," "promote resentment toward a race or class of people," "are designed primarily for pupils of a particular ethnic group," or "advocate ethnic solidarity instead of the treatment of pupils as individuals" (HB 2281). The banning of ethnic studies programs in Arizona signals a significant shift in the education of Latinxs in the United States, once again positioning cultures such as those of Mexicans and Native Americans as insignificant and "other" in a dualistic mode of thinking that promotes Anglocentric ways of knowing and culture above all others. Such splitting of identity and cultural communities serves to keep Latinxs in their oppressed state, thereby ensuring that they remain powerless in their education curricula.

Especially problematic in recent years, since the global pandemic of 2020, have been the numerous discriminatory and racist laws aimed at erasing minority histories, literature, critical race theory (CRT), and diversity programs. Though the death of George Floyd, a black man, at the hands of an overzealous, racist white police officer, Derek Chauvin, spurred mass protests in the United States and beyond, the years since have seen backlash against changes aimed at eliminating racist and discriminatory practices. Since the death of Floyd and the height of the Black Lives Matter movement in 2020, most recently, many states, including Texas, have banned CRT, as well as teaching about racism, from K–12 classrooms. Though the term *critical race theory* is not explicitly used in the bills passed, nine states have passed what is termed anti-CRT state legislation (Ray and Gibbons). In addition to anti-CRT legislation, states such as Texas have also passed laws colloquially called anti-DEI laws, such as Texas's SB 17, which close DEI offices at public universities. The impact of this on public higher education includes hindering schools and their administrators from fostering a diverse and welcoming campus. Last, Texas and Florida have led the way in banning books from K–12 classrooms and libraries. Specifically, HB 900 bans "sexually explicit" books from school libraries and classrooms while also requiring that stores selling books to schools establish a rating system to assess the degree of "sexual" content in books (Solomon). The books that are targeted usually contain content mentioning or about issues surrounding LGBTQIA+ individuals or racism/discrimination. In each case, such laws demonstrate that racism and discriminatory practices continue to permeate our society and are infringing upon K–12 and college education, thereby resulting in censorship and the erasure of literature, history, and diverse pedagogical curricula and practices in the classroom. Though the 1990s and early 2000s saw a rise in addressing diversity in the school, we have much work to do as the backlash against those strategies emerges more forcefully in classrooms today at the K–12 and university levels.

2

PROBLEMATIZING THE U.S. EDUCATION SYSTEM AND ITS IMPACT ON LATINA IDENTITY, EPISTEMOLOGIES, AND FAMILY

While chapter 1 provides a brief historical account of the impact of racist and assimilationist pedagogies on Latinx students, this chapter[1] will review how Latinas cope with the U.S. education system. A close examination of Latina literature and testimonios reveals the difficulty Latinas find in retaining ties to their cultural epistemologies once introduced to the assimilationist pedagogies of U.S. schools. As discussed in chapter 1, the U.S. school system sometimes rejects their cultures, ethnicities, and communal epistemologies. Such rejections have created regret, alienation, confusion, and fear of failure. These feelings stem from the disconnection between Latinas, their families, and their cultural communities because students desire to invite their families and communities on their education journey. However, K–12 schools and especially academia are not spaces in which the family and knowledge of Latinx cultural communities are readily accepted. In addition, Latinas also experience alienation from their communities when their families require that they attain

---

1. Parts of this chapter and chapter 3 were originally published as "'The Fourth Choice': Forging the Future of Chicanx Mother/Daughter Relationships Through Storytelling and the Path of Conocimiento in Erika Sánchez's *I'm Not Your Perfect Mexican Daughter* and Barbara Renaud González's *Golondrina, Why Did You Leave Me?*," in *Label Me Latina/o*, vol. 8, 2018.

an education yet remain loyal to their cultural traditions, which may often conflict with the newfound knowledge gained in school. In this way, Latinx families strive to stay connected to their children without adapting to the multiple epistemologies their students have begun to acquire.

I focus my research on the alienation that Latinas experience once they are introduced to the assimilationist, patriarchal methods of the U.S. education system as portrayed by the protagonists of contemporary Latina literature and testimonios. In this chapter, I ask how the U.S. school system affects a Latina's identity and her interaction with family and community. What can Latinas do to balance the formal education they achieve in school with cultural knowledge, educación? I argue that part of the answer emerges when Latinas encounter the education/educación conflict, as discussed in chapter 1. This conflict reveals an imbalance between U.S. systemic schooling and cultural knowledge, leading to alienation from school and their home or cultural community. I posit that an answer to this conflict could lie in adopting a mestizaje of epistemologies within the third space of education, where Latinas employ the weaving of cultural and institutional epistemologies and identities. I specifically examine Latina identity rather than that of Latinxs as a whole to address the multiple oppressions encountered by Latinas due to their ethnicity and gender and the unique experiences they encounter as women within both their cultures and Anglocentric patriarchal society.

DEFINING THE EDUCATION/EDUCACIÓN CONFLICT

Before I offer a possible remedy to the education/educación conflict, it is necessary to understand the dilemma at various levels in higher education and K–12 and the education pathway between K–12 and college.[2] My reasons for focusing on the effects of higher education on Latinas and their ties to their cultural communities relate to Latinx high school students and the increasing dropout rates of Latinx as they attempt to progress beyond high

---

2. Though I acknowledge that many Latinxs experience this conflict, not all of them experience it in the same way, if at all. In some rare cases institutional education has provided a way for Latinas to reconnect to their culture, history, and language, as indicated by scholars such as Edén E. Torres in *Chicana Without Apology*.

school and through the educational pipeline. Though these numbers have improved in recent years for Latinx students, inequities persist for Latinx trying to achieve higher education degrees, and we have yet to realize the full impact of COVID-19 on this particular group. However, universities and colleges continue to deal with decreasing enrollment rates. HSI researcher and expert Gina García reveals,

> The Latinx population is one of the largest racialized groups in the United States, with 56.6 million people identifying as Latinx in 2015, or 17.6% of the population . . . This representation is rapidly increasing, with predictions that the Latinx population will reach 119 million by 2060, or 29% of the population . . . This population increase is simultaneously reflected in postsecondary enrollment. In fall 2015, three million of the 17 million students enrolled in undergraduate programs in the United States self-identified as Latinx, which is 17.6% of the total undergraduate population, making them the second largest racialized group in higher education, behind white students . . . Despite the growing presence of Latinxs in higher education, their postsecondary completion rates are inequitable compared to their white counterparts. (72)

Though enrollment has undoubtedly increased for Latinx students, as García points out, low retention and graduation rates persist. Current research on the college completion rates of Latinx students reveals that 28 percent of Latinx adults (twenty-five and older) have obtained an associate degree or higher as of 2021 ("Latino College Completion"). At the same time, since 2014, we have seen a significant decrease in dropout rates from Hispanic high school students. Pew Research data reveals a 32 percent drop from 2000 to, in 2014, a 12 percent dropout rate among students from ages eighteen to twenty-four. However, this rate is still higher than that of black (7 percent), white (5 percent), and Asian (1 percent) students (Krogstad). It is also important to note that since that time, COVID-19 has significantly impacted the education pipeline for all students, but especially for Latinxs. Current research indicates that enrollment at postsecondary institutions in the United States increased from 2000 to 2019, from 1.5 million to 3.8 million. However, the COVID-19 pandemic brought a decrease in enrollment. By the fall of 2020, colleges saw a decrease in student enrollment by 640,000 (Mora). As for high school dropout rates, Hispanics' dropout rate has seen a new low since 2016, despite the COVID-19 pandemic. Numbers reveal that in 2016, "the Hispanic dropout rates was 10% ... with about 648,000 Hispanics ages 18 to 24—out of more than 6.5 million nationally in that age group—not completing high school and not enrolled in school. Just five years earlier, the rates had been 16%" (Mora). Though these low high school dropout rates and high college enrollment numbers indicate positive upward trends for Hispanic students, it is essential to note that Hispanics continue to lag behind other races and ethnicities in other academic measures, as discussed previously.

When it comes to the specific breakdown of the Latina education pipeline, research in the last decade indicates percentages of dropout rates similar to those of the overall Latinx community; Chicana social psychologists Aída Hurtado and Mrinal Sinha explain, "a recent study by the American Association of University Women Educational Foundation documented Hispanic women and men had a higher high school dropout rate (30%) than Blacks (11.1% for males and 12.9% for females) and Whites (9.0% for males and 8.2% females)" (149). Current research analyzed by Excelencia in Education utilizing the U.S. Census Bureau's data reveals that as of 2021, 27 percent of Latinas had obtained a high school diploma, and 14 percent of the 27 percent had received a bachelor's degree, thus revealing that the number of Latinas completing each level of schooling continues to remain low ("Latinas"). Such information shows that as Latinas attempt to move through the educational pipeline, the representation of Latinas in college and graduate school begins to dwindle. Studies such as this reveal statistics regarding Latina success rates in school based on grades and dropout rates but do not answer why Latinas have trouble in school.[3]

Though there are many diverse reasons why Latinas and Latinxs encounter higher high school dropout rates and lower college graduation numbers, I argue that we may find a solution to some of the identity issues Latinas face by examining literature and testimonios written by contemporary Latinas

---

3. According to the 2010 census, Latina students in college have surpassed the number of Latinos. The 2010 census and Hispanic Pew reports indicate that though the number of Latinas in college has increased, the representation of Latinos continues to dwindle. Pew reports indicate that "college-age Hispanics accounted for 1.8 million, or 15% of the overall enrollment of 12.2 million young adults in two-or four-year colleges in 2010," signaling a 24 percent increase in Hispanic enrollment (Fry). Despite these increases, Hispanics continue to lag behind white and African American college students.

to reveal how protagonists and writers deal with the education/educación conflict as a reflection of the more significant issues at work in the realm of education and pedagogy. Works such as the Latina Feminist Group's *Telling to Live*, Gloria Anzaldúa and Cherríe Moraga's *This Bridge Called My Back*, Gloria Anzaldúa and AnaLouise Keating's *This Bridge We Call Home*, and Barbara Renaud González's *Golondrina, Why Did You Leave Me?* are only a few examples of texts that reveal the complex identity conflict experienced by Latinas throughout the decades. I also dedicate one of my final chapters to research conducted with some of my current students as they provide their education testimonios discussing these issues. I argue that this conflict often results in school failure, alienation from family and culture, and uncertainty regarding one's identity. Edén Torres describes this conflict when she observes that

> one of the reasons Mexican Americans—Native Americans and African Americans as well—cannot be compared to other "immigrant" groups has to do with the traumatic histories to which [authors such as Aletícia] Tijerina and Anzaldúa among others refer. We did not choose to leave our homelands as many European immigrants have, nor elect to be absorbed into the dominant culture through forced assimilation, which is a kind of brutality against the spirit. Our indigenous ancestors made no request to be incorporated into two or three national states through violence. As Mexican settlers we did not choose to lose our language and culture, to be included (yet excluded) in the original social experiment known as the United States of America. As a result of this material reality, we have been made relatively powerless over and within public and private institutions that directly affect our lives—churches, schools, governments, and the structures of commerce. (20)

The result of the forced assimilation and participation of Latinxs in U.S. society and institutions such as schools is to blame for the identity conflict and alienation they encounter daily. Especially significant is Torres's assertion that assimilation is a "brutality against the spirit" because this methodology requires that Latinas split or, in some cases, completely dismiss parts of their identities. After all, specific identity markers are privileged over others. Julissa Arce echoes Torres's assessment of assimilation and its dire effects on Latinx communities as she asserts that "assimilation is not a road to belonging, but rather the carrot America dangles in front of immigrants, Latinos, and other people of color, an unreachable goal to keep us fighting for the single place at the podium rather than spending our energy creating spaces where we don't have to compromise who we are to fit in" (9). In noting these observations about assimilation, we must consider how such strategies directly impact Latinas in the school system, mainly because assimilation is specifically designed as a strategy to ensure that Latinas do not obtain "success," sever ties with their cultures and communities through the adoption of assimilationist strategies, or both.

We can examine the school system by utilizing CRT to understand the methods of assimilation schools employ. CRT and, more specifically, Latino and Latina critical legal theory describe how the Anglocentrism of schools affects Latinas' school success, ties to their cultural community, and identities. Theorists such as Aída Hurtado, Jeanett Castellanos, Dolores Delgado Bernal, and others have examined the education/educación conflict, though they utilize CRT. Others have attempted to meld CRT with theories such as Chicana third space feminism and literary theories to discuss various aspects of Latina identity. However, I contend that this conflict requires further examination and research, especially as we find ourselves as educators and scholars on the front lines fighting against a return to systemic racial discrimination in schools. I argue that part of the solution to the education/educación conflict that Latinas encounter as a result of this systemic racial discrimination lies in the exploration of Latina literature and testimonios using both literary theories and CRT. The combination of both literary theories and CRT allows for a more extensive exploration of the literature written by and about Latinas, which often chronicles or observes essential issues Latinas face, including those in school. At the same time, combining literary analysis with CRT expands how one might examine the problems faced by Latina students by looking at the structural and institutional discriminatory practices that Latinas have encountered in the school system. Several examples of these systemic discriminations are observed by noted legal scholar Albert H. Kauffman in his article "Latino Education in Texas: A History of Systematic Recycling Discrimination." Kauffman—an activist for the Mexican American Legal Defense and Education Fund, an organization focused on protecting the legal civil rights of Latinxs—details the various instances of systemic discrimination encountered by Latinxs throughout history, including the exclusion of Mexican American students from schools in states such as Texas, the segregation of Mexican American students from their Anglo counterparts, tracking systems, and discriminatory English language learner programs designed to increase segregation (878). Therefore, I examine Latina literature and testimonios utilizing Chicana third space feminism and CRT to develop my theoretical approach, which deconstructs Latina identity as it relates to their experiences with the U.S. education system and exposure to multiple epistemologies.

I define the education/educación identity conflict as the inability to balance institutional epistemologies attained in the U.S. system of education with the educación of the home, thereby leading to uncertainty about one's identity. I use Lilia D. Monzó and Robert S. Rueda's work with Latinx students and their understanding of educación to reveal how the education/educación conflict emerges. Monzó and Rueda explain that Latinx students come to school with a specific knowledge of the type of educación they will receive. For Latinx students, educación is more than simply attaining knowledge in the classroom and building relationships with teachers to attain that knowledge in a safe environment where students can discuss the more extensive world issues that schools may bring up. Strictly adhering to academic content and creating a distinct line between teacher and student is detrimental to the Latinx student, who expects to form a relationship because this is the familiar model used at home. Specifically, Latinxs in the home environment often gain knowledge from elders, such as their parents or grandparents, with whom the student already has a relationship. Moreover, Monzó and Rueda argue that educación is learning through caring, which involves "recognizing their social position; being willing to discuss the issues that concern these students and validating the diverse knowledge they bring to the classroom, including their language and experiences. Such a caring relationship would lead to greater responsivity and intersubjectivity and ultimately to more effective learning contexts" (442). In other words, Latinx students expect that their teachers are invested in more than their academic success, as their families are. Latinx students expect their teachers to care about who they will become as valued members of society, establishing caring relationships and academic success.

In *Sentipensante (Sensing/Thinking) Pedagogy: Educating for Wholeness, Social Justice and Liberation*, Laura Rendón also takes note of the disconnection established by teachers' lack of concern for their students as whole beings. In reflecting on her own experiences with the U.S. school system, Rendón explains that "no one asked [her] to reflect on the meaning and purpose of what [she] was learning" (3). She adds that "no one asked [her] to write about what [she] knew best ... life experiences and what [she] had learned from them" (3). For Rendón and countless other Latina students, the classroom is often a foreign place with unfamiliar and daunting material. Rendón asserts that her relationships with her teachers were virtually nonexistent and lacking, and the knowledge she gained was far removed from her own experiences. According to schools and teachers, such distance was necessary because, as Rendón argues, it ensured discipline (3). Thus, Rendón's experience with K–12 education allows her to critique the education system and the teachers who distanced themselves from her. She calls for an engaged teacher caring about students' well-being beyond academics to address this discrepancy. Though Rendón's experiences are reflective of the U.S. education system during the fifties, sixties, and seventies, it is essential to note that similar observations persist to this day, as demonstrated through core curricula courses, including history and literature, that are noninclusive of diverse cultures, races, and ethnicities, and the standardized testing environment in several states such as Texas.[4] My final chapters will provide more information on the effects of these problems on Latinas' experience in higher education.

In contrast to educación is the institutional education implemented by U.S. public schools. Institutional education relies on assimilationist, patriarchal, and racist curricula and pedagogy. Examples of assimilationist pedagogy are included in Sofia Villenas and Donna Deyhle's critique of the U.S. education system. They reveal the U.S. education system's desire to eliminate bilingual education in California in recent decades and the insistence that English remain the sole language of learning. Villenas and Deyhle note that the "history and perspectives of Chicanos/as and Mexicanos/as are completely left out of the curriculum" (421).[5] In addition to the U.S. education system's

---

4. Though Texas now allows for Mexican American studies courses at the high school level, these classes are elective and not mandatory. In discussing discriminatory literature and history courses presently I am referring to the standard, core curriculum that every Texas student must take, which does not include Mexican American studies courses as mandatory to the curriculum.

5. Though my work primarily focuses on the effects of the U.S. education system on Latinas and Chicanas, I must acknowledge that the Anglocentric ideology that permeates our school system also negatively affects other minority students, such as African Americans and Native Americans.

not including the histories and literature of minority students, Rendón also notes that educators are "woefully unprepared to deal with these issues [hate crimes, school violence, and suicidal behaviors] within the confines of an educational system that devalues social, emotional, and inner-life skill development" and that these personal issues have been further exacerbated since the global pandemic (4). Rendón explains that a new model of educating must be developed, one that focuses on the "balance between our inner life of intuition, emotion, and sense of meaning and purpose, and the outer world of action and service" (4). Many of these problematic elements of our school system originate in the disconnect that teachers, curricula, and schools establish between themselves and their students. I argue these problematic elements have become more pronounced in states such as Texas, where teachers are not allowed to teach about racism or discrimination, to bring in literature that directly addresses these issues, or to correct historical narratives that might shed light on things such as systemic racism and its connections to slavery. Though Pew reports indicate that there has been an increase in Latina enrollment in college institutions, the secondary and postsecondary graduation rates still lag behind those of Anglo and African American students. In addition, as Latinas attempt to move up the education pipeline, their numbers decrease. Graduation rates become even more complex when one contemplates the differences between U.S.-born Latinas and new Latina immigrants. Such studies demonstrate that the education/educación conflict may be more complex for new immigrant Latinxs. Though such differences exist between U.S.-born Latinas and new Latina immigrants, they share similar problems of assimilation to Anglocentric pedagogy, including socioeconomic issues and language barriers, which often lead to low success rates in school.[6] The issue of education for newly arrived Latinx immigrant students will grow exponentially as we see an influx of immigrants coming to the United States from various Latin American countries via Mexico following the pandemic. However, this is not the focus of this research. Part of the conflict these immigrants and U.S. Latinas encounter lies in the binary thinking dominating school curricula and pedagogy.

---

6. For the purposes of this study, I focus on Latina protagonists and writers representative of second- and third-generation immigrants and those who have resided in the United States for a few generations.

TRANSITIONING BEYOND BINARY THINKING

Epistemologies of the U.S. school system privilege binary thought, in which specific identity markers are deemed superior, universal, and the "norm" compared to others. Examples of these dichotomies include Anglo versus Latinx, male versus female, English versus Spanish, heterosexual versus queer, upper class versus working class, and education versus educación. Such binaries establish the "superiority" of Anglos, males, the English language, heterosexuals, the upper class, and education over Latinxs, females, the Spanish language, queer people, the working class, and educación. Such classifications establish who is and is not privileged, according to the U.S. school system and society. Latina and Chicana students must then contend with institutions that enforce these binaries, thus rejecting many of their identities. Alternatively, they are forced to split up their identities, often discovering the need to choose those qualities that schools and society reveal will help students succeed and become part of the privileged. Such pedagogy and structuring of schools continue the divide-and-conquer strategy utilized by the European colonizers against the Indigenous population from the outset of colonization. It serves to split Latinas from their cultural communities, their families, and themselves, thereby establishing the individual/communal binary in which the individual is privileged, further asserting the American ideology of rugged individualism in which one strives to achieve their American dreams whatever the cost, which may lead to what scholars call "abyssal thinking."

Andreotti, Ahenakew, and Cooper discuss the concepts of "sides" and "abyssal thinking" about epistemologies and the dominance of one kind over another. The authors summarize Boaventura de Sousa Santos's idea of "abyssal thinking" as "a system of visible and invisible distinctions established through a logic that defines social reality as either on 'this side of the abyssal line' or on the 'other side'" (Andreotti et al. 42). Andreotti, Ahenakew, and Cooper further assert that binaries support abyssal thinking, which dictates what is universal and what is not. In the case of Latinas and their educational experiences, certain kinds of knowledge and ways of learning become "normalized" and establish the "norm" for certain binaries' (either/or) ways of thinking. One such example is the English/Spanish binary in the school system. Historically, Spanish has not been allowed as a language that students may utilize to communicate, let alone in their reading and writing within schools. Therefore, the U.S. school system establishes abyssal thinking in the context of an English/

Spanish binary, which asserts that English is the universal and "normal" way of communicating in school and that Spanish is not, allowing room for punishment if one deviates from the "norm." Therefore, Andreotti, Ahenakew, and Cooper argue that universality is established based on the "invisibility of ways of knowing that do not fit parameters of acceptability" established in their example by law and science (42). However, this is also true in the realm of K–12 and academia. Certain abyssal lines dictate which epistemologies are the acceptable "norm" and which are deemed irrelevant.

For example, *female, Latina, working class,* and *queer* are perceived by most of society's epistemologies as negative identity markers, and as such, they are also classified as oppressions, identities Latinas must work to overcome, especially if they are to "succeed" in K–12 and academia. Such binary systems allow and encourage the age-old colonization plan of dividing and conquering in institutions such as the U.S. school system. This divide-and-conquer strategy works to keep many Latinas from their cultural communities, forces them to assimilate, or leaves them confused about their identities. Latinas become separate individuals who feel that their struggle against and navigation through the education system is a solitary one when it could be a collective endeavor. We can define the education/educación conflict as this confusion of identity and alienation experienced by Latinas once they encounter oppositional epistemologies represented by their cultural and institutional education systems.

Andreotti, Ahenakew, and Cooper assert that breaking free from the binary thought process or restricted way of thinking in which one epistemology dominates another is necessary. This can occur in multiple ways, as seen historically throughout literature such as Rudolfo Anaya's *Bless Me, Ultima*. In Anaya's text, the protagonist, Antonio, grapples with spiritual belief systems that seem contradictory, such as his questioning of Catholicism versus the Indigenous belief systems represented in the story of the golden carp. By the end of the novel, Antonio is left considering whether there is a way to merge both types of spirituality and ways of thinking about the world, to "take the llano and the river valley, the moon and the sea, God and the golden carp—and make something new... 'Papá,' I asked, can a new religion be made?'" (247). This example demonstrates how multiple epistemologies can be woven together and accepted, breaking free of specific restrictive binary ways of thinking. Other scholars have discussed similar strategies that allow them to weave between and among multiple epistemologies. María Lugones discusses her concept of "world traveling," which she describes as something practiced out of necessity by women of color in the United States; she argues that as outsiders, women of color have "acquired flexibility in shifting from the mainstream constructions of life where she is more or less 'at home.' This flexibility is necessary for an outsider, but it can also be willfully exercised by the outsider or by those at ease in the mainstream" (3). This is a similar concept to that of Chela Sandoval's differential consciousness, a shifting between identities depending on the situation one finds oneself in, much like the gear shifter and clutch of a car one must manually shift and thus adapt depending on the positionality one finds oneself in (*Methodology* 15). Similarly, I add to these concepts by embracing and weaving multiple ways of knowing, a mestizaje of epistemologies, which Latinas can adopt once they break free of binary thought processes.

A MESTIZAJE OF EPISTEMOLOGIES: A STRATEGY TO COPE WITH THE EDUCATION/EDUCACIÓN CONFLICT

I derive my concept of a mestizaje of epistemologies from multiple scholars who utilize the idea of mestizaje in their research. Using the work of Gloria E. Anzaldúa, Rafael Pérez-Torres, Dolores Delgado Bernal, Venetia June Pedraza, Lourdes Alberto, and Suzanne Bost, I arrive at a new understanding of mestizaje; however, it is the work of Anzaldúa that helps me situate my main argument in conversation with other mestizaje scholars.[7]

I utilize and add to Anzaldúa's notion of mestizaje by focusing on this in-between space where the weaving of seemingly contradictory identities and epistemologies come together. Anzaldúa discusses the idea of mestizaje by analyzing what she calls mestiza consciousness. La mestiza, Anzaldúa argues, is "in a constant state of mental nepantilism, an Aztec word meaning torn between ways, *la mestiza* is a product of the transfer of the cultural and spiritual values of one group to another. Being tricultural, monolingual, bilingual, or multilingual, speaking a patois, and in a state of perpetual transition" (*Borderlands* 100). Part of being in a state of perpetual transition includes the multiple epistemologies and identities Latinas must engage in, especially within institutions such as the U.S. school system. Therefore, I argue that the mestiza can be torn between multiple educational epistemologies,

---

7. I'm also indebted to the work of Teresa Córdova, Leslie G. Espinoza, and Cristina Beltrán.

specifically those of her home/communal cultures and the Anglocentrism that dominates learning institutions.

Anzaldúa further argues that for Chicanas and Latinas to embrace a weaving of multiple ways of knowing, they must first break free of binary thought through what she refers to as mestiza consciousness. According to Anzaldúa, mestiza consciousness is also the awareness that a mestiza develops once she begins to accept a "tolerance for ambiguity" represented by her multiple and often conflicting identities, cultures, and ways of thinking: "the new *mestiza* copes by developing a tolerance for contradictions, a tolerance for ambiguity. She learns to be an Indian in Mexican culture, to be Mexican from an Anglo point of view. She has a plural personality, she operates in a pluralistic mode—nothing is thrust out, the good the bad and the ugly, nothing is rejected, nothing abandoned. Not only does she sustain contradictions, she turns the ambivalence into something else" (101). I add to and expand on Anzaldúa's notion of developing a tolerance for ambiguity via a mestizaje of epistemologies. I argue that this tolerance can be applied in both the school and home setting in respect to identity and epistemology when Latinx students become aware of the education/educación conflict not as a binary split but as a balancing of these seemingly contradictory ways of knowing. The mestizaje of epistemologies operates in the same way as the mestiza consciousness when Latinx students learn how to balance their home/cultural epistemologies with school ones, accepting that one can retain ties to one's cultural identities but also "succeed" academically in Anglocentric schools if consciousness of this tolerance is achieved. This consciousness-raising further allows one to break free of the binary way of thinking described by Anzaldúa and others. This break occurs through reflection and assertion of strategic epistemologies that embrace ambiguity, as seen in the literature and testimonios written by Latinas.

In adding to and expanding on Anzaldúa's notion of mestizaje, it is necessary to look to her sources, including José Vasconcelos and his idea of *una raza mestiza, una mezcla de razas afines, una raza de color—la primera raza síntesis del globo* (Anzaldúa, *Borderlands* 100). While this concept of a united race that embraces all races as one seems like a positive goal, it is necessary to complicate this notion of mestiza or mestizaje and the history behind the term. I begin this context with the conquest of the Caribbean islands now known as Cuba, Puerto Rico, and the Dominican Republic. With the arrival of the Spanish to the islands, racist ideologies emerged, including their beliefs about racial superiority. During this period, Latin America was "divided into a caste society, also referred to as a *system of stratification*. This system was based on skin color and phenotypical characteristics" (Chavez-Dueñas, Adames, and Organista 6–7). This system allowed the Spanish to control political, social, and economic power while impoverishing Indigenous populations and African groups brought to the Americas as enslaved people. The colonial period lasted roughly three centuries, ending in 1830, by which time each Latin American country had gained independence from Spain. During the postcolonial era, the foundation of white superiority continued and flourished through the development of mestizaje. Chavez-Dueñas, Adames, and Organista note that this ideology was one "whereby everyone was deemed to be of mixed descent" and was one of the strategies employed by the Spanish to "deemphasize privileges associated with phenotypically White characteristics" (8). In addition to this strategy, the goal of mestizaje was to assimilate indigenous and African people into a culturally homogeneous society with the belief by the Spanish that with time, mestizaje "would lead to the disappearance of indigenous and African cultures from Latin American society" (9). The history of mestizaje thus reveals an attempt to "whitewash" and assimilate both Indigenous and African colonized people with the eventual goal of disconnecting or completely erasing these cultures and races.

Over time, the mestizaje concept shifted and was adopted by Chicano and Chicana scholars and theorists during the Chicano movement and well into the 1980s and beyond. Though the term initially emerges with a problematic context and history, it can and has been reimagined and recovered to highlight the positive ways we might contemplate identity and epistemologies. Noted Chicano scholar Rafael Pérez-Torres discusses the significance of mestizaje in understanding Chicanx identity in his seminal text *Mestizaje: Critical Uses of Race in Chicano Culture*: "mestizaje occupies a valued position in Chicana critical discourse because, as a descriptive term and a cultural practice, it helps embody the idea of multiple subjectivities. Moreover, mestizaje signals the embodiedness of history. As such, it opens a world of possibilities in terms of forming new relational identities. At the same time, it signals how the body is tied to a colonial history of racial hierarchy whose power relations already constrain and guide the body" (3). As Pérez-Torres argues, Chicanas eventually utilized the term *mestizaje* to understand the complexity of Chicanx identity, one that embraces all aspects of identity: the Indigenous, Afro-mestizx, Anglo, and beyond. At the same time, Pérez-Torres acknowledges the complicated history of the term *mestizaje* by noting the long history of colonial violence. In invoking this idea of a mestizaje of epistemologies, I hope to reimagine and reenvision the term *mestizaje* as one that acknowledges the balancing of multiple identities and ways of knowing our world, without succumbing to binary ways of thinking or ignoring the hierarchy that mestizaje once embraced. Instead, I suggest that the origins of mestizaje as a tool of colonization may be reenvisioned to reject and resist this idea of racial purity, positing it as a social construct that can be reimagined.

In considering the erasure of the Indigenous, using the term *mestizaje* becomes especially important and complex when one deliberates a Latina's identity conflict regarding Indigenous aspects of herself and epistemologies that she may not recognize and whether she has a right to embrace them. Latinas are often faced with the choice of embracing their Indigenous identity, denying it, or finding ways to balance their Indigenous genealogy alongside their family's and culture's history of colonization. This is especially problematic because Anglocentric schools would like to ignore the Indigenous identity of Latinas, and many parents and families, due to hundreds of years of colonization efforts, also ignore or are ignorant of possible Indigenous ties. Latinas also find themselves unable to feel as if they can legitimately claim their Indigenous identity because of their Latinx cultures and resistance from some Native Americans themselves. This uncertainty emerges, as Ana Castillo reveals, because the "denigration of our [Mexicanx and mestizx] indigenous blood has been so pervasive that few of us, especially in the past, have claimed our lineage" (8). The inability to accurately identify which tribes Latinas may or may not belong to has severed ties to Latinas' Indigenous identity. This dilemma is further complicated, as Anzaldúa indicates, when Latinas discover that "within us and within *la cultura chicana,* commonly held beliefs of the white culture attack commonly held beliefs of the Mexican culture, and both attack commonly held beliefs of the indigenous culture. Subconsciously, we see an attack on ourselves and our beliefs as a threat and we attempt to block with a counterstance" (*Borderlands* 100). As each aspect of one's identity is attacked, especially in educational institutions, the feelings of uncertainty and alienation grow, leading to the need to choose between aspects to survive and succeed. Part of the problem may also lie in the fact that accepting one's Indigeneity includes accepting the abuse and racism that "la India" has endured. Suppose Latinas can overcome their inability to claim Indigenous identity. In that case, they may be opposed by Native Americans who claim they are simply appropriating Native American culture and identity if this is not their current lived experience.

Cherríe Moraga and Celia Herrera Rodriguez also explore Latinas' reluctance to claim Indigenous identity from a Chicana perspective. Moraga and Rodriguez, like Castillo, note that from the perspective of "some less informed North American Indian activists, Xicanos hold no rights to their Indigenous identity by virtue of their Mexicanism.[8] This perception is aggravated by the fact that most of the Mexicans in the United States and México have historically denied (and been denied) their Native identities" (7). To counter such assertions, Moraga and Rodriguez argue that Chicanxs and Latinxs must contemplate their position within a society that ignores part of their history. They must form a "living critical consciousness about their land-based history" (7). At the same time, the history of Indigeneity and mestizaje in Mexico especially reveals another strategy employed by scholars such as José Vasconcelos to invoke a "multicultural utopia in contemporary Mexican and Mexican American culture"; however, this nationalist project reveals "the political project of mestizaje established the boundaries of indigenous identity in the national imaginary even as actual indigenous were the target of assimilation projects" (Alberto 112). Bearing this historical context in mind, one must contemplate how Latinas and Chicanas can navigate their Indigenous histories and genealogies in a way that acknowledges their ongoing presence and the effects that colonization continues to perpetuate on Indigenous peoples in contrast to the relative "ease" with which Latinas and Chicanas may or may not be able to embrace their own Indigenous identities. Lourdes Alberto, a Zapotec Indigenous scholar, further argues that in contemplating Indigenous identity as it relates to Chicanxs especially, one must consider that "the identification of indigenous presence should not be a sign of residual indigenous culture; rather, indigenous culture should be recognized as the dominant culture attached to actual villages, places, and people" (119). Rather than assuming an Indigenous identity, critical consciousness of how Indigeneity has been usurped and appropriated to suit a country's or culture's needs must first be contemplated.

---

8. Moraga and Rodriguez explain that they spell *Xicana* and *Xicano* (*Chicana* and *Chicano*) with an *X*, indicative of the Nahuatl spelling of the *ch* sound, to "indicate a re-emerging política, especially among young people, grounded in Indigenous American belief systems and identities" (xxi).

Such consciousness may allow Latinas to come to terms with their multiple identities, including the Indigenous aspects of their selves.

While considering the complexity of Indigenous identities and epistemologies as part of Chicana and Latina student identity, it is necessary to acknowledge the diversity accompanying the concept of mestizaje, including identifying as Afro-mestizaje. Though Anzaldúa does not directly address the idea of Afro-mestizaje, it is essential to contextualize her writings and scholarship. She is initially writing about her life experiences in the Rio Grande Valley, a place dominated by Mexicans and Mexican Americans, with very little African American presence. At the same time, while she invokes mestizaje as a blending of Spanish, Indigenous, Mexican, and Anglo cultures and identities, she does so in direct response to the scholarship and activism of the 1960s during the Chicano movement, thereby resituating how Indigenous identity might be utilized to bring Chicana efforts into the forefront of these efforts. Theresa Delgadillo's discussion of spiritual mestizaje helps us to understand how Anzaldúa revises narratives of the Chicano movement and Indigenous identity:

> *Borderlands* thereby distances itself from both Chicano and Mexican nationalist projects that police sexuality and gender as Anzaldúa reopens the term *mestizo/a* and *mestizaje* for interrogation based on their historical meanings. Since the mestizo/a subject has historically been disenfranchised, marginal, and impure, Anzaldúa claims that space outside of the center and asserts it as the space from which new cultures and identities emerge, a process to which she emphatically subscribes, although in the contemporary situation with a different set of cultures. (13)

Anzaldúa, in her reworking of these concepts to acknowledge those who have been disenfranchised in movements such as the Chicano one of the sixties, calls out its sexism and patriarchal nature while calling for a new space where new cultures and identities can be developed. Though Anzaldúa wrote in the 1980s, *Borderlands* was published in 1987 and attempts to speak to the elements of the Chicano movement that were highly problematic. Since that time, Anzaldúa's ideas continue to be considered as the idea of mestizaje transforms. They must now directly address Afro-mestizaje and Latinx mestizaje, given our current political climate and new understandings of how to address systemic racism, especially in schools, via antiracist pedagogies.

While Anzaldúa's discussion of mestizaje includes Indigenous identity and culture, it seemingly elides African presence. In the case of Latinas who might be from or have ties to Caribbean islands such as Cuba, Puerto Rico, and the Dominican Republic, among others, it is essential to note the historical differences they encountered, especially regarding colorism and white superiority. Suzanne Bost notes that "the *mestizaje* originated by Spanish colonization clashed with U.S. race segregation. While the United States attempted to implement legalized divisions between black and white, the different racial composition of Puerto Rico led to less visibly apparent structures of racism" (194). We see examples of this complexity of race in many instances of Latina literature and education testimonios written by Puerto Ricans and Dominicans, including Loida Maritza Pérez's *Geographies of Home*. In the case of the protagonist, Iliana, her experience with the education/educación conflict is markedly different from that of the Chicana protagonist of *Golondrina, Why Did You Leave Me?* because Iliana is Dominican and therefore Afro-mestizaje and Afro-Latina. Not only must Iliana contend with an education system that discriminates against her because of ethnicity, but she is also subjected to systemic racism because of the color of her skin, as we see in the opening pages of the novel *Geographies of Home* when Iliana, a Dominican American, decides to return home after experiencing countless experiences of overt racism, including finding racially charged messages on her dorm room door (1). More contemporary novels with Afro-Latina protagonists, such as Xochitl González's *Anita De Monte Laughs Last*, further reveal how the education/educación conflict continues to be encountered.

Such examples demonstrate the need to contextualize and restate the unique history of Caribbean mestizaje, such as the Dominicans and Puerto Ricans, and how that remains with Dominican American and Puerto Rican students and their experiences in school. Shirley Anne Tate and Ian Law's chapter in *Caribbean Racisms: Connections and Complexities in the Racialization of the Caribbean Region*, titled "Mixing, Métissage and Mestizaje," explains that in considering mestizaje in the Spanish-speaking Caribbean, the idea of "*blanqueamiento* policies have produced nations which see themselves as white but are irrevocably mixed... When mixing is acknowledged in the Dominican Republic it is the Taínos who are referenced so that rather than the nation's heritage of African enslavement, a submerged Indigeneity, and foregrounded Europeanness are the basis for citizenship" (59). Thus, in the case of the Dominican Republic, the nation relies on this attempt to whitewash and blend the Indigenous with the white, thereby erasing ties to Africa, often resulting in contemporary antiblack racism. In invoking this idea of mestizaje as it applies to epistemologies, it is important to contextualize and keep in mind the history of colorism. However, I argue that the term *mestizaje* can be recovered in such a way that acknowledges Afro-mestizaje cultures and identities, especially within an educational and epistemological context, if we remain conscious of its origins while considering how a mestizaje of epistemologies can balance the seemingly contradictory histories of the oppressor/oppressed, cultures, and identities.

Mestizaje may further be recovered as a mestizaje of epistemologies if the consciousness of its colonial history, steeped in colorism and racial hierarchies, is part of the balancing of this education and educación epistemologies, primarily via the stories and knowledge of such experiences as passed down by families and the analysis of the connection between mestizaje and contemporary colorism. In much the same way that Anzaldúa sought to rectify and redress problematic elements of mestizaje as utilized during the Chicano movement to emphasize Chicanx Indigeneity and nationalism while silencing Chicana voices, I seek to redress her idea of mestizaje by applying it to epistemologies that are shared and exchanged without erasing or favoring one epistemology over another. Instead, I argue that a mestizaje of epistemologies calls for balancing seemingly contradictory home and cultural epistemologies with those of school, thus inviting our communities to the classroom.

AWARENESS OF POSITIONALITY BETWEEN MULTIPLE EDUCATION IDEOLOGIES AS CONSTRUCTED BY SOCIETY

I argue that to achieve a mestizaje of epistemologies, one must do so in the third space of education. The third space of education is an in-between space, similar to Anzaldúa's concept of nepantla. However, the difference is that Latina students who encounter the education/educación conflict find themselves between multiple epistemologies and identities about learning. Specifically, the third space of education arises when Latinas realize that the assimilation, racism, and sexism of their schools instill both a sense of not belonging and one of belonging. Once Latinas reach the awareness that binary thought dominates the pedagogies and methodologies of K–12 and academia, Chicanas and Latinas can transition to the third space of education.

This idea of not belonging and belonging is also felt in the home environment due to exposure to the Anglocentric epistemologies of schools. Thus, Latina students are thrust into the third space of education where they are aware of belonging to and not belonging to their cultural and institutional epistemologies and identities. In this third space, they learn how to shift and navigate between the spaces of their institutions and schools. This is also where they learn how to reject dualistic thinking and privileges and begin to form new ways of thinking about society and education beyond simplistic notions of right and wrong ways of learning. Part of that realization includes understanding that education need not be an individual's task; instead, it can be a communal effort. In this way, Latina students may invite their families and cultural communities to expand and adapt their epistemologies while doing the same in school. This can occur in the same way that family stories and knowledge are passed on from generation to generation at the kitchen table. In the same way, Latina students may converse with their families and communities, passing along the knowledge they attain at school and vice versa.

Shifting into the third space of education occurs when one knows the positionality between multiple educational ideologies. I argue that Latinas begin to achieve such understanding when they experience what Anzaldúa describes as the path of conocimiento. Anzaldúa explains that the path starts with a "rupture or a traumatic experience that causes a mestiza to reflect upon her life, identity, and position in the world, while also thrusting her into the third space" ("Now Let Us" 544). In the context of education, Latinas begin their path of conocimiento when they experience trauma related to contrasting educational ideologies. For example, Anzaldúa's reflection on her own experience in the realm of education demonstrates how it begins to complicate her identity further:

> Bereft of your former frame of reference, leaving home has cast you adrift in the liminal space between home and school. In class, you feel you're on a rack, body prone across the equator between the diverse notions and nations that comprise you. Remolinos (whirlwinds) sweep you off your feet, pulling you here and there. While home, family, and ethnic culture tug you back to the tribe, to the Chicana indigena you were before, the Anglo world sucks you toward an assimilated, homogenized, whitewashed identity. Each exhorts you to turn your back on other interpretations, other tribes. You face divisions within your cultures—of class, gender, sexuality, nationality, ethnicity. You face both

entrenched institutions and the oppositional movements of working-class women, people of color, and queers. Pulled between Chicano nationalists and conservative Hispanics. Suspended between traditional values and feminist ideas, you don't know whether to assimilate, separate, or isolate. ("Now Let Us" 548)

This trauma is experienced from encountering educational ideologies that are different from those of the home culture. Contact with academia and the attempt to incorporate Indigenous ways of knowing, as Anzaldúa attempts to do, become problematic because there is a need to translate such knowledge into "the dominant language, logic and technologies in ways that are intelligible and coherent . . . to readers and interpreters in the dominant culture" (Andreotti et al. 44). Once again, attempting to adhere to binary thought's "superior" aspects creates conflict. However, the consciousness of such differences coupled with a desire to retain ties to one's culture compels them to move into the third space of education, beyond the first and second spaces represented by the dominant Anglocentric culture and their own.[9] The experienced trauma propels an individual into a third space of education, where they are forced to reflect and question their life, identity, dualistic thinking, and educational ideologies.

In this third space of education, Chicanas and Latinas realize that they must struggle to retain and maintain a mestizaje of epistemologies, including the institutional knowledge of U.S. schools and the cultural understanding of their homes and communities. To balance these multiple epistemologies, Latina students must "re-situate themselves in different knowledge systems

---

9. The concept of the third space was originally explored by Homi Bhabha and is derived from his notion of hybridity. Smadar Lavie, explaining the differences between Gloria Anzaldúa's and Homi Bhabha's understanding of multiple spaces and hybridity, refers to Bhabha's construction of "hybridity as mimicry in the form of hegemonized rewriting of the Eurocentre," which reveals a "fragmented Otherness in the hybrid." On the other hand, Lavie argues, Anzaldúa's explanation of hybrids reveal that they "delve into their past [and] it need not be either essentialized nostalgia or the salvaging of an 'uncontaminated' precolonial past." Instead, a "reworking of the past exposes its hybridity, and to recognize and acknowledge this hybrid past in terms of the present empowers the community and gives it agency" (68). Thus, the difference emerges in the agency that is attained as individuals versus community.

(including the experience of language/stories as metaphor), as well as re-situating themselves in their bodies, emotions, and spirits" (Andreotti et al. 46). This concept is strikingly like Walter Mignolo's discussion of "border crossing," in which he discusses the need to displace the epistemic privilege of the hegemony by "subsuming the first set of terms in the paradigm into the second by making of it a locus of enunciation as legitimate as the first" (942). It is not enough to acknowledge that a balance between epistemologies must occur; Latina students must genuinely learn how to belong in and between various knowledge systems. Latinas must learn how to weave such epistemologies together so that both knowledge systems are equally validated in the multiple environments of the home and school. Such validation and acceptance represented by the weaving of mestizaje of epistemologies also legitimize Latinas' and Chicanas' identities at home and school. This legitimization is necessary to ensure a shift beyond the education/educación conflict into a space where healing can occur, paving the way for the next step in transforming the U.S. education system to one that validates and embraces cultural educación.

A mestizaje of epistemologies is not simply about focusing on the education/educación conflict but is also about the healing process it entails. Yes, the conflict is why a theory such as a mestizaje of epistemologies is needed; however, strictly focusing on that aspect offers no solutions. A possible solution emerges through healing, which can occur through weaving together multiple epistemologies and identities that the education/educación conflict has severed. Such healing emerges through reflection, questioning, and emerging consciousness that arises via the path of conocimiento.

I argue that by following the path of conocimiento, Latinas can become aware of their positions and identities at home and school. They become aware that racism and oppression exist in different forms both at home and at school. At this moment, Latinas shift into nepantla, an in-between space, where they become two people at once, the person before the shift and after (Anzaldúa, "Now Let Us" 544). While in this in-between space, Latinas begin to "examine the ways [they] construct knowledge, identity, and reality, and explore how some of your/others' constructions violate other people's ways of knowing and living" (544). Through this examination, students may gain agency and become empowered enough to contest the Anglocentric epistemologies and pedagogies thrust upon them in the school system.

Nepantla emerges in spaces such as the physical borderlands, as inhabitants who dwell there cannot claim a place on either side of the border but are in between spaces at once. Anzaldúa writes about the U.S.-Mexican border as "*una herida abierta* where the Third World grates against the first and bleeds. And before a scab forms it hemorrhages again, the lifeblood of two worlds merging to form a third country—a border culture" (*Borderlands* 25). Part of belonging to that border culture involves an awareness of one's position where multiple worlds, identities, and epistemologies collide or meet. Similarly, Latinas encounter the assimilationist and patriarchal techniques utilized by the U.S. school system, which thrusts them into nepantla, the in-between space that Anzaldúa explains emerges when two worlds merge to form a third—border culture. In education, Latinas are forced into nepantla, which is formed when the epistemologies of their home and society collide to create a third space of education. In this third space of education, multiple epistemologies form a mestizaje of epistemologies, a balance of various ideologies that allow Latinas to retain ties to their culture while succeeding in school. This can occur in cultural and institutional environments when a blending of education and educación methodologies emerges through sharing family stories, speaking cultural languages, and reading literature and history written by Latinas. It is in this space that Latinas engage in Chela Sandoval's notion of "strategic essentialism" to "'speak back' to hegemonic powers" by emphasizing "generosity, reciprocity, solidarity, relationality, interdependence, abundance, immanence and respect for the gifts of internal and external difference. This respect guarantees a 'space to speak from' ... where each can offer one's (different) contribution and help each other learn ... by offering perspectives from different angles" (*Methodology* 49). This speaking back can occur in several ways, including the sharing and telling of Latinas' education stories, literature, history, and testimonios.

To resolve this identity dilemma, Latinas must attain awareness of their position between multiple educational ideologies. This awareness allows them to move into the third space of education, where Latinas can survive and multiple educational ideologies coexist. In the third space of education, institutional epistemologies and educación are equally balanced once Latinas begin to practice applying a mestizaje of epistemologies to their academic and cultural lives. In the third space of education, Latinas know their position between multiple epistemologies. Latinas become conscious that their subjectivity has been constructed by society in such a way that they are placed at the margins compared to the hegemony. It is necessary, as Norma Alarcón puts it, to "[break] out of ideological boundaries that subject her [Chicanas and Latinas] in culturally specific ways, and not crossing over to cultural and political areas that subject her as 'individual/autonomous/neutralized' laborer" (254).

Therefore, the third space of education allows Latinas to question their subjectivities and begin to alter them. Similarly, Anzaldúa's discussion of the Coatlicue state reminds Chicanas, and I would argue all Latinas, that "every increment of consciousness, every step forward is a *travesía*, a crossing . . . Knowledge makes me more aware; it makes me more conscious. 'Knowing' is painful because after 'it' happens I can't stay in the same place and be comfortable. I am no longer the same person I was before" (*Borderlands* 70). Reaching consciousness of one's racialized and sexualized position, especially in learning environments, propels one beyond into a third space, where a new subjectivity can be formed, a subjectivity that allows the use of multiple epistemologies as a survival strategy in various worlds and cultures.

In the third space of education, Latinas begin to alter their subjectivities once they question the dominant ideologies of the U.S. school system and their cultural epistemologies. Such questioning also involves the contestation of dominant, Anglocentric ideologies of the U.S. school system through the reinscription of Latinas' histories and stories. Of particular importance is the method by which Latinas reinscribe their histories through writing/telling their stories, which then results in empowerment and healing for the author and the reader.

ALTERING SUBJECTIVITIES: QUESTIONING AND CONTESTING DOMINANT IDEOLOGIES IN U.S. SCHOOLS

To balance the multiple ideologies presented by U.S. institutions of learning and our cultural environments, it is necessary to question and contest the dominant ideologies of schools, which may allow for the alteration of one's subjectivity. Latinas must use the tools of the U.S. school system, such as literary traditions and historical research, to reinscribe themselves into history while breaking through the silences forced on them.

Part of reinscribing oneself back into history begins with what Emma Pérez proposes is the time lag that occurs between a colonial and postcolonial state: the decolonial imaginary, "that interstitial space where differential politics and social dilemmas are negotiated" (*Decolonial Imaginary* 6). Pérez focuses on the activities and words of Chicanas, Mexicanas, Indias, and mestizas as they "intervene to do what [she calls] sexing the colonial imaginary, historically tracking women's agency on the colonial landscape" (7). Women's stories are removed from the margins and placed in the center of the decolonial imagination. Latinas attempt to retain ties to their culture, community, and identity by exploring and sharing their stories.

As Pérez notes, we must examine the stories and histories of Chicanas (I would add Latinas and all women of color) and focus on "taking the 'his' out of the 'story,' the story that often becomes the universalist narrative in which women's experience is negated" (*Decolonial Imaginary* xiv). Pérez argues that we must uncover the histories of women who have long been silenced to finally allow their voices to emerge. Latinas contest the histories that have excluded them while also attaining agency through the emergence of their histories and voices, which emerge through rejecting the privilege of Anglo, patriarchal histories. Inclusion of the histories of women is critical when addressing the education/educación conflict that many Latinas experience. Since one solution to the conflict is a mestizaje of epistemologies, it is necessary to place equal importance on the histories and stories of Latinas in addition to institutional education, thus rejecting the binary that insists Latina history is insignificant.

Part of reinscribing Latinas' stories and identities back into history also involves adapting Chela Sandoval's concept of differential consciousness. Latinas achieve a mestizaje of epistemologies by attaining what Sandoval refers to as an awareness of one's position within multiple worlds, a differential consciousness. Sandoval further explains that differential consciousness was first acknowledged as a survival strategy by women of color in response to the 1970s white feminist movement. Women of color recognized that their needs were not addressed in the white feminist movement, and therefore, they created their groups and moved between them. She describes the activity of weaving between and among multiple oppositional ideologies as "'differential,' insofar as it enables movement 'between and among' ideological positionings" (*Methodology* 58–59). Differential consciousness is a survival tactic developed by women of color to cope with their existence in the third space. Women of color use differential consciousness to move between oppositional ideologies and identities depending upon the situation they find themselves in.

I add to Sandoval's concept of differential consciousness by arguing that Latinas engage in it not only once awareness of their position within multiple worlds occurs but specifically once their understanding of their place between many epistemologies arises. I contextualize Sandoval's concept of differential consciousness between the cultural and institutional environments where Latinas are exposed to seemingly oppositional epistemologies. This exposure to oppositional epistemologies forces Latinas to shift between those environments and, more importantly, weave together mestizajes of epistemologies. This shifting and weaving occurs once Latinas experience a traumatic encounter such as racism or sexism, discrimination, or a sense of not belonging in the home or school environment, usually related to the oppositional epistemologies of these spaces.

Differential consciousness is one method that mestizas can employ when they become aware of stressful, dangerous, or problematic situations. Sandoval provides a simplified definition of differential consciousness by explaining that it is like shifting gears in a car: whatever the road/situation calls for will depend upon the type of response a mestiza must employ to survive (Sandoval, "U.S. Third World Feminism" 14). The metaphor of shifting gears is also helpful in understanding how such near-automatic shifting occurs in a third space of a mestiza's narrative. In the case of the narratives I engage with, the Latina protagonists automatically shift into a third space of education when they encounter assimilationist pedagogies in institutions of formal learning. This shifting allows them to choose to succeed in such institutions while retaining ties to their cultural knowledge once back in the home environment. The development of a differential consciousness allows Latinas to weave between the epistemologies of their cultural community and institutions of learning.

Part of developing a differential consciousness also includes what Anzaldúa calls la facultad. Anzaldúa describes la facultad as the "capacity to see in surface phenomena the meaning of deeper realities, to see the deep structure below the surface. It is an instant 'sensing,' a quick perception arrived at without conscious reasoning. It is an acute awareness mediated by the part of the psyche that does not speak, that communicates in images and symbols which are the faces of feelings, that is, behind which feelings reside/hide" (*Borderlands* 60). I argue that Latinas develop la facultad as a survival tactic in institutional education when caught between multiple educational epistemologies. La facultad allows Latinas to perceive the colonial, racist, and sexist practices utilized by the U.S. school system beforehand. Once Latinas experience this awareness, they are propelled beyond the world in which they were unaware of such oppressions. Latinas are unable to move into a world where they can contest oppression. Thus, they exist in a third space of education where they can live and negotiate between both worlds. In the third space of education, Latinas may develop a mestizaje of epistemologies where they use knowledge from their institutions of education and educación to resist the oppressions of their old world and work to attain agency in the third space and beyond.

This chapter has outlined the various literary and educational theories I have used to develop my theory of a mestizaje of epistemologies. In the following chapters, I will critically analyze the protagonists and writer of *Golondrina, Why Did You Leave Me?* and excerpts from various anthologies by women of color. The protagonists of *Golondrina* develop a mestizaje of epistemologies in the third space of education as a response to the racist assimilation experienced in school and a desire to retain ties to their families and cultural communities. Each of the protagonists and writers of these literary works either engage in the steps involved in utilizing a mestizaje of epistemologies in their lives or begin to realize that such a theory is necessary to rectify the education/educación conflict they encounter.

3

NAVIGATING THE EDUCATION/ EDUCACIÓN CONFLICT IN *GOLONDRINA, WHY DID YOU LEAVE ME?*

While chapter two thoroughly defined the education/educación conflict and the theories I use to examine it, chapter three will focus on developing and applying the literary/educational theory I will utilize to analyze Barbara Renaud González's *Golondrina, Why Did You Leave Me?* (2009). I will demonstrate how the protagonists of *Golondrina* employ my theory of a mestizaje of epistemologies as a solution to the education/educación conflict. I will first identify how the education/educación conflict significantly impacts the identities and communal/familial ties of the protagonists in *Golondrina*. I argue that the protagonists of *Golondrina*, Lucero and Amada, encounter the problems accompanying the education/educación conflict once exposed to the U.S. education system. This conflict results in feelings of alienation from their families, cultures, and communities. Lucero (the daughter) begins resolving the education/educación conflict once she realizes her position between multiple ideologies. Such awareness occurs in the third space of education, where Lucero learns how to balance institutional education with educación by adopting a mestizaje of epistemologies.

Golondrina is set in various towns throughout Texas and on the border between the United States and Mexico. The story first follows the journey of Amada García, a young Mexican woman who decides to leave her abusive husband and young daughter behind to seek a life for herself in the United States. Once in the United States, she marries, has children, and encounters the struggles of being a Mexican in the United States, including poverty, discrimination, and racism. Her story is narrated by her daughter, Lucero, who attempts to reconcile the narratives of her Texas Mexican father with that of her Mexican mother while trying to understand her identity as a Mexican American woman.

Golondrina is told from a uniquely female, Mexican American perspective. The story is framed by Lucero's uncertainty about her identity, which results from the Anglocentric epistemologies of her learning institutions coming into opposition with her home/cultural ideologies when she finds herself "called" home. The story begins with Lucero returning to her home and mother as an adult. Once at home, Lucero asks her mother to share their family stories, resulting in Lucero's evaluation of her own subjectivity and how the academic experience has impacted her and her family. Though the narrative does not focus solely on Lucero's schooling experiences, there is no doubt that the formal institutions she attends signal a shift in consciousness via a path of conocimiento, discussed in previous chapters. Lucero enters the first stage of conocimiento, one that allows her to contemplate her positionality in school, society, and home, once she is discriminated against at school because of her race and gender. As a result of such persecution, Lucero experiences a transition and awareness of her positionality, which Anzaldúa refers to as "un arrebato," a jolt from the familiar, a shifting between worlds ("Now Let Us" 546). Such awareness includes the shattering of the belief that assimilation is the only solution to the oppression Lucero endures. This shift in consciousness is the second step once Lucero encounters the path of conocimiento, in which she contemplates her place in the world. Once this awareness is achieved, Lucero begins to contemplate her understanding of the world and where such societal constructions emerge within a third space of education; a shifting between epistemologies occurs between the school and culture in this place. This shifting and negotiating between cultural and institutional ways of knowing can emerge as a mestizaje of epistemologies, a balance of cultural and school epistemologies and identities. Thus, because of such traumas, Lucero begins to examine her life by analyzing her family's histories and stories. I argue that Lucero discovers the need to balance the epistemologies of her school with her culture, which allows her to embrace her multiple identities.

GOLONDRINA, WHY DID YOU LEAVE ME? AND A MESTIZAJE OF EPISTEMOLOGIES

Lucero begins to embrace her multiple identities, beginning with her family story and questions about how her mother crossed the border from Mexico to the United States.[1] The act of questioning signals the beginnings of Lucero's growing awareness, which is needed to balance multiple epistemologies. This balancing begins in a particularly significant kitchen setting, as Amada performs domestic chores such as cleaning and cooking. As Amada begins her story, Lucero notes that her mother is reluctant to tell it: "I can tell she's sorry that I'm just like her. I'm an exile just like she's been all her life, only from a different side of the river. So, I keep going" (3). Though Amada reluctantly begins to relay her life experiences to her eager daughter, Lucero notes the stories behind the silences accompanying her mother's narratives. In those silences, scholar Cristina Herrera notes that "Amada *does* communicate with her daughter, conveying complex, empowering maternal knowledge that is transmitted through her engagement of household tasks such as ironing, folding laundry, washing dishes, or cooking" (443). Through such actions, Amada also conveys essential knowledge to her daughter, including, as Herrera notes, "critical tools such as a resistance, the importance of maintaining cultural identity, and love of learning," which Herrera refers to as "maternal knowledge" (443). I argue this is part of Lucero's educación, or cultural knowledge. As Amada works and imparts both her verbal narratives and the "maternal knowledge" transmitted through her labor, Lucero begins to take note of her and Amada's unique positionalities in society. Lucero immediately notes that she and her mother cannot fully belong to Mexico or the United States because of society's definitions of their identities. Amada's inability to acculturate marks her

---

1. González retells the legend of the golondrina (swallow) as a preface to her text: At the beginning of time, God offered a prize to the one who could travel the world and tell the story best of what he or she saw. Many wanted to leave but were afraid of the dangers of an unknown journey. Crow left first but got interrupted with some carrion and returned without seeing hardly anything. Then Swallow left. Swallow took many months in returning, and when everyone thought Swallow had died, the bird appeared one day telling of an infinity of things that had been seen on the whole trip there and back. As a prize, God gave the swallow the gift of changing countries.

as different, as not belonging (according to Anglo-Americans) to the United States because of her lack of English skills, brown skin, and culture.

In contrast, Lucero's ability to acculturate into Anglo society, but not entirely, also marks her as different. At the same time, she cannot fully claim a Mexican identity because she was born and grew up in Texas, knows English and some Spanish, and has been educated in the United States. Gloria Anzaldúa speaks of this dilemma as she explains, "Chicanos and other people of color suffer economically for not acculturating. This voluntary (yet forced) alienation makes for psychological conflict, a kind of dual identity—we don't totally identify with the Mexican cultural values. We are a constructive collaboration of two cultures with various degrees of Mexicanness or Angloness" (*Borderlands* 85).

Because Lucero is forced to acculturate, she becomes alienated from her family and culture, especially from her community's epistemologies. This sense of alienation occurs primarily due to Lucero's exposure to the epistemologies of her formal U.S. education, which leads to the development of the education/educación conflict. The result of this conflict is Lucero's inability to identify fully with the epistemologies of her home or school. The education/educación conflict forces Lucero to privilege the epistemologies of her school over cultural knowledge. This privilege is also a part of the binary thinking that the U.S. school system attempts to instill within Lucero, thus creating a conflict for her because she refuses to accept this epistemology readily due to her mother's teachings. Instead, she has to negotiate between multiple cultures and, as I argue, balance various epistemologies to resolve this dilemma.

Lucero encounters the education/educación conflict once she enters the U.S. school system, which prompts her to examine identity further to resolve it. Lucero begins to address her education/educación conflict once she is propelled into the third space of education, where she can adopt and accept a mestizaje of epistemologies. Lucero is first thrust into the third space of education in the same way that Anzaldúa argues that one enters the path of conocimiento. Because Lucero feels alienated from her home culture due to her newly developed English skills and her inability to communicate fully at school, she cannot fully belong to her home or school cultures. Instead, she is thrust into an in-between space, a type of nepantla. According to Anzaldúa, in nepantla, one is always "in a constant state of mental nepantilism" (*Borderlands* 100). Venetia June Pedraza further clarifies Anzaldúa's notion of nepantla by explaining that nepantla is a "new realm where third space mestizas/os begin to see the subject/object duality, the 'us' and 'them' dichotomy. While in this *Nepantla*, this third space, mestizas/os come into an awareness of their marginality, and they begin to understand the need for social change" (93). Anzaldúa further explains that in nepantla, "transformations occur in this in-between space, an unstable, unpredictable, precarious, always in transition space lacking clear boundaries. Nepantla es tierra desconocida, and living in this liminal zone means being in a constant state of displacement—an uncomfortable, even alarming feeling" (*Interviews* 243). Nepantla is also the first space or stage in the path of conocimiento, which one enters when encountering some trauma, whether it is mental, physical, or spiritual.

Anzaldúa's description of the path of conocimiento helps to describe Lucero's experiences with systemic and overt racism once at school. Anzaldúa explains that trauma, such as the type Lucero encounters when she is rejected both at home and school, often catapults one into nepantla. Since Lucero's trauma is a direct result of her encounter with U.S. institutions of learning and the culture that dominates them, I refer to this type of nepantla as the third space of education, a place between multiple epistemologies. Lucero's experience in the third space of education can be described using Anzaldúa's observation of such an experience:

> in this liminal transitional space, suspended between shifts, [where] you're two people, split between before and after. Nepantla, where the outer boundaries of the mind's inner life meet the outer world of reality, is a zone of possibility. You experience reality as fluid, expanding, and contracting. In nepantla you are exposed, open to other perspectives, more readily able to access knowledge derived from inner feelings, imaginal states, and outer events, and to 'see through' them with a mindful, holistic awareness. Seeing through human acts both individual and collective allows you to examine the ways you construct knowledge, identity, and reality, and explore how some of your/others' constructions violate other people's ways of knowing and living. ("Now Let Us" 544)

In this third space, Lucero becomes two distinct people: the individual she was before she entered the U.S. school system and the person she now is, after she has endured oppression and survived. This in-between state is a third space because Lucero cannot truly belong to the first space represented by her cultural epistemologies, nor can she comfortably occupy the second space of institutional ways of knowing. The alternative to the first and second spaces is the third space, a melding of the first two spaces and the epistemologies that dominate them.

This position allows Lucero to examine how she has constructed knowledge, her identity, and reality according to the epistemologies taught by her family and school. The third space of education allows Lucero to reflect on the oppression she has endured because U.S. institutions of learning violate the ways of knowing and living that she has learned from her parents and culture. Specifically, Lucero's brown skin, her culture, and her initial inability to speak English make her feel alienated at school. Lucero begins to note that her school is composed of a dualistic way of thinking in which her identity markers signal her "inferiority." The fact that Lucero is Chicana, has darker skin, initially speaks only Spanish, and wants to belong marks her as "inferior" according to Anglocentric ideologies and epistemologies.

Once Lucero begins to encounter trauma after trauma due to this lack of belonging both at home and school, she can become conscious of her identity as she perceives it based on Anglocentric norms, which privilege binary ways of thinking. Such realizations especially become evident once Lucero encounters arrebatos that force her to question and reflect on the familiarity of her surroundings, including the belief that such oppressions are the "natural" way of society. As Lucero reflects on the trauma experienced in school, she notes that the other Mexican children refuse to assimilate because "they don't want to belong like I do, they have no chance, but at least they belong to each other. They tell me I'm the stupid one, for pretending to be a gringa, and now the *mexicanos* are beginning to hate me, too. The crazy thing is I'm beginning to hate them back, they just don't know it's the gringos I hate even more for making me hate them" (González 95). Though Lucero wishes to assimilate and tries her best, she realizes that she still does not belong to the Anglo world. As a result of her attempted assimilation, Lucero experiences hatred from the Anglos, who reject her because she is Mexican American and thus considered "inferior" according to the dualistic ways of thinking, and the Mexicanos because they feel she is a sell-out. In addition, Lucero begins to hate both the Anglos and Mexicanos back because both groups continue to contribute to the problematic dichotomies she has already started to question, thus causing her further confusion regarding her identity. Thus, Lucero is in this liminal state, nepantla.

Lucero becomes further aware of her position between multiple epistemologies once she is forced to abandon her Spanish words in favor of English ones. This also leads to awareness that an Anglocentric society constructs her subjectivity. She, too, has begun to accept that English is better than Spanish and, therefore, more privileged. Because Lucero is Mexican American and the school system, including her teacher, is Anglo, the pedagogy and curriculum are Anglocentric; Lucero does not have a chance to learn about her culture's history, nor is she able to express herself accurately due to the language barrier. Scholars Villenas and Deyhle reveal how Anglocentric pedagogy directly affects Latinas such as Lucero; they argue "the rich knowledge, beliefs, and worldviews of Latino and Mexicano/Chicano communities are not validated, let alone taught" in school (421). The insistence on utilizing impersonal and nonpersonal techniques in the classroom also leaves Lucero with no one to turn to, especially as she begins to forget the Spanish language. Lucero describes the alienation she feels as she attempts to ask for help: "*Frijole* eater, greaser, dirty, stupid, *gobacktoMexico spic*. How do I say they call me these names because of you, Mami! Or the way my classmates laugh at my clothes and skin and even my hair, as if I was some monster, uglier than Frankenstein... Every day they look at me as if I don't belong here, as if I don't deserve to be in school with them, as if they want to break me into little pieces like my Spanish words already are" (González 95). Lucero understands that she cannot go to her mother for help because she no longer possesses the language to do so and believes her mother could never understand what she is enduring. This alienation is further explored and clarified if one applies Laura Rendón's pedagogical theories: instead of being concerned with students' subjective realities and working with a moral ethic of caring that fosters positive relationships between teachers and students, many schools are focused on detachment, nonpersonal content, and impersonal and objective language. This results in many students feeling that who they are and what they represent are not valued in school (35). Detachment is especially felt when race/ethnicity comes into the picture, as in Lucero's case. Lucero knows she could never turn to her teachers or classmates because they mock her; she reveals the persecutions endured at school, explaining, "They've already broken the other Mexican kids, some of them pretend they don't speak Spanish anymore, and the others who won't learn English are failing, just like they want us to. And though I'm polite, they still hate me, still call me those names. I'm not dumb like they say, either" (González 94–95). Each of these incidents leads to confusion of identity for Lucero because acceptance of her culture ensures further alienation and oppression. At the same time, the assimilationist pedagogy of her school pushes her further from her family.

The initial inability to speak English also separates Lucero from her classmates, revealing that she does not belong because she only speaks Spanish. Thus, Lucero experiences alienation from her classmates, teachers, and school environment. Lucero doesn't even attempt to consider bilingualism, perhaps because, as Dolores Delgado Bernal reveals, "bilingualism often continues to be seen as 'un-American' and considered a deficit and an obstacle to learning" ("Critical Race Theory" 112). Because of this, Lucero is not encouraged to retain her native language. Lucero's exposure to school and the English language gradually begins to conquer the Spanish of her home and family. The result of her education, then, is regret at not being able to communicate with her family, namely her mother, or the Mexican children at her school. A confusion of identity accompanies these feelings of alienation and regret. Namely, she is experiencing the education/educación conflict.

This alienation also emerges because, as Michel Foucault explains, institutions such as schools attempt to mold students' bodies into what I refer to as the figure of the ideal student, similar to the military's desire to create the figure of the perfect soldier (135). Foucault's idea of docile bodies can be extended to include the concept of docile minds when discussing Latinas such as Lucero and their experiences in school. I add to Foucault's use of the concept of "docile bodies" and argue that this extends to students' minds as schools attempt to mold, transform, and improve them through assimilation. However, when discussing docile minds and Latina students, I contend that school techniques such as assimilation and acculturation call for a complete transformation of the mind so that the student's thinking complies with that of the Anglocentric hegemony. In the case of Latina and Chicana students such as Lucero, the school and its representatives attempt to eradicate their culture by transforming their cultural ways of thinking and perceiving the world via assimilation.

Because of assimilation and the invalidation of cultural epistemologies that accompany it, Latina/Chicana students such as Lucero face persecution when they attempt to counter assimilationist pedagogies. Such persecution causes Lucero and others in similar circumstances to question the legitimacy of their cultural knowledge, therefore leaving students' minds open to manipulation. Through this transformation, the hegemonic culture can gain cultural and disciplinary control over the docile minds of Latinx students. Further control is exerted over Lucero here because the school system has split her identity and connection to her community and family, leaving her with a "docile mind" that can be manipulated and molded to accept assimilation and the belief that her cultural knowledge is insignificant. Such strategies are reminiscent of the divide-and-conquer strategy previously mentioned in chapter 2.

Anzaldúa further complicates Foucault's discussion of control exerted over the soldier's body as she describes the dilemma that the mestiza must endure in an Anglo culture. Anzaldúa explains that "within us and within *la cultura chicana*, commonly held beliefs of the white culture attack commonly held beliefs of the Mexican culture, and both attack commonly held beliefs of the indigenous culture" (*Borderlands* 100). These attacks primarily occur in the classroom, where the Latina body struggles against the control that the Anglo culture attempts to exert. Thus, it becomes pretty complicated to overcome the challenges embodied in this concept of the figure of the ideal student. To demonstrate her worth, Lucero must work hard in school to the point that she emerges at the top of her class academically. This can also be read as an act of differential consciousness: Lucero chooses to do well in school to survive, though she must yield to the assimilation strategies employed by the teachers. However, her intelligence gets her nowhere with either the Mexican or Anglo children. Instead, they both begin to hate her; the Mexicans insist she is nothing more than a gringa, while the Anglos despise her Mexican heritage.

This education/educación conflict is further complicated when Lucero is at home and realizes she has begun to lose the ability to communicate with her mother. Lucero describes the pain of being unable to hold on to the Spanish language: "I'm not saying very much because somewhere between the first and fifth grade I lost some words, and I don't know where they went. The words are from Mami, and trying to find them hurts. And I'm afraid I'll never see them again, and then what" (González 94). Lucero realizes she is losing ties to culture and family as she begins to succeed in school and speak better English. She feels conflicted and wants to succeed in school while remaining linked to her family, language, culture, and community. As Lucero describes the music her mother enjoys hearing, she reveals the "notes high and low, up and down, sideways, they slide by so fast, they remind me of all the Spanish words that have left me, so I can hardly breathe" (88). Lucero is then confronted with choosing between multiple identities and epistemologies because the world in which she is entrenched reveals the impossibility of belonging to both worlds.

Lucero also reaches consciousness regarding her position between multiple epistemologies at home and within her own culture. This primarily emerges through her mother and father's conflicting stories and histories. Lucero observes that when Amada occasionally mentions her *india* blood, it is to the chagrin of her husband; she also notes that her grandmother feared the mark of the india because it was a terrible reminder of one's heritage. Amada informs her daughter that her mother hated her "because she was born with that telltale blotch of purple on the sole of her left foot, the Indian stain, proof she was from those people who refused to die, those people, almost everyone came from but wanted to forget, and couldn't because their mothers were Indians too" (González 32). Amada's husband, Lázaro, expresses his disdain for Indian identity when Amada attempts to proclaim their Indian heritage to her children proudly. Though Lázaro constantly denies his Indian heritage, Lucero finds herself wondering about her Indian identity. When Lázaro asks his children if there are any more Indians, Lucero thinks "about how people always ask me when we go to Oklahoma what tribe I belong to. Wish I knew" (115).

Lucero's inability to claim her Indigenous identity can also be attributed to the Anglocentric pedagogy and discourse utilized by the school. Specifically, the idea that "we are all immigrants" is often used to deny "Chicanos/as and their Mexican relatives a claim to the Southwest (Aztlan) as their homeland and thus their indigenous or native status in the area now held as the United States. Second, it denies Spanish, a language that was protected under the Treaty of Guadalupe-Hidalgo, its status as an indigenous language of the United States (before the English language). Third and most insidious, the 'we are all immigrants' claim also works to assert the inferiority of 'brown-skinned' Latinos/as" (Villenas and Deyhle 421). As a result of the "we are all immigrants" attitude, Chicanas such as Lucero must struggle with claiming their land, language, and Indigenous identities. While Amada affirms her family's Native American heritage and Lázaro denies it, Lucero is left to decide on her own what to claim as her identity. Though she claims a Native American identity, she expresses pain at not being able to accurately identify which tribe her family may have come from. Lucero's identity is further complicated by her father's revelations that his great-great-great-grandfather was a red-haired Irishman who married a Mexicana; his great-grandmother, Camelia, married a mulatto from Louisiana; and Gertrudis (Lázaro's great-great-great-grandmother) was a mestiza with "spanish skin but Indian in the places you can't see," thus emphasizing the mestizaje of cultures Lucero is from (González 113).

One of the ways Lucero attempts to contest the Anglocentric epistemologies thrust upon her by her school is by reinscribing her mother's story and her own into history. In choosing to tell her story, Lucero rejects the versions of history that ignore women. Emma Pérez's discussion of Chicana history explains that it is necessary to be "concerned with taking the 'his' out of the 'story,' the story that often becomes the universalist narrative in which women's experience is negated" (*Decolonial Imaginary* xiv). Lucero alludes to the stories that are often hidden and forgotten as she explains the importance of storytelling in her family:

> Mami taught me the best story sometimes takes a lifetime to tell, that's why you have to tell it over and over until you get it right. The best story, like a quilt she said, is made from scrap pieces of cloth, old buttons, leftover thread, and don't forget the worn outs and *manteles*, "*¿verdad, mijita?*" That's where the real story is, she said, just look for it in the cabinet where everything's stored away and forgotten. And that's how I'm telling you this story, finding the hand-carved jewelry box I brought her once from Hawaii. (González 7)

Lucero's realization that she must share her mother's story and her own reveals the beginning of her desire to contest the lack of women's, especially Chicanas', stories throughout history. Lucero's storytelling directly contests the privileges of Anglocentric histories, making room for those once deemed insignificant stories. Amada's story is significant because her story, like many others, has been relegated to the margins, and these are often the stories "previously unheard, rebuffed, or underestimated," according to Pérez (*Decolonial Imaginary* xv). Pérez further explains it is the

> voices of women from the past, voices of Chicanas, Mexicans, and Indias [that] are utterances which are still minimized, disregarded, even scorned. And time, in all its dialectical invention and promise, its so-called inherent progress, has not granted Chicanas, Mexicanas, Indias much of a voice at all. We are spoken about, spoken for, and ultimately encoded as whining, hysterical, irrational, or passive women who cannot know what is good for us, who cannot know how to express or authorize our own narratives. (*Decolonial Imaginary* xv)

By asking her mother to relay her story, Lucero finally gives her mother the voice and freedom she desperately desires. Lucero must help her mother achieve her voice because she represents Mexican, immigrant, Chicana, and Indian women. Amada's voice and her story have been suppressed in multiple ways throughout her life, first by her mother, especially when Amada wishes to go to school "but there is no money," and then by her former husband, Sapo, who prevents her from telling her story because her duty is to "say nothing" (González 11, 18). Last, Amada's story is often silenced by Lázaro's stories and his insistence that she should forget Mexico and the Spanish language. Despite the silencing that Amada must endure, it is her daughter, Lucero—a name that means "light, but more than that, more like a necessary light in darkness"—who will break it by telling her mother's stories (105). This is especially important within the context of education because women, specifically Latinas, are often silenced in the classroom through various disciplines such as literature and history, which continue to be male centered.

Amada's story is exceptional and cannot occupy "traditional" spaces; instead, she must relay her experiences from a space representative of many cultures, worlds, languages, and encounters. Because Amada cannot fully belong to Mexico or the United States, her story goes untold in these places, allowing room for it to be told through her daughter in the third space of education. This third space of education involves storytelling and writing while requiring Amada and Lucero to form a differential consciousness as they reflect on their life experiences. Chela Sandoval argues that when people are marginalized in dominant societies, just as Amada and Lucero have been, a process of deconstruction of dominant ideologies takes place. Amada's and Lucero's exposure to the oppositional epistemologies of the U.S. school system and their cultural environment has caused them to question their positionality in both spaces. In short, Amada and Lucero begin to question why their home and school cultures reject them, why the Anglocentric epistemology is privileged over their cultural ways of knowing, and why their identities as Chicanas are rejected in both spaces. Such awareness and questioning emerge primarily through the act of storytelling.

Both women choose to weave between epistemologies rather than submit to one epistemology or identity over another. This is especially evident in Lucero's decision to relay her family's story because she decides to tell her own story; she is contesting Anglocentric master narratives. She employs the English language to share this story, suggesting an acceptance of certain aspects of the Anglocentric epistemology. These acts can be defined as engaging in differential consciousness because both women choose to relay their experiences using the English language and writing, both assimilation tools, to tell their stories. Amada deconstructs her position within the dominant Anglo society by offering her story to her daughter. In turn, Lucero does the same when she provides the reader with the interweaving of her family's stories. From a uniquely Chicana perspective, the decision to relay her family's story contests the privileging of Anglocentric, patriarchal, individualistic ways of thinking. By bringing in the stories of both sides of her family and from each perspective, Lucero further acknowledges the community aspect of storytelling, thereby reestablishing a connection to the communities she has disconnected from because of Anglocentric, assimilationist pedagogies. In this way, Amada and Lucero can find a voice in a society that has often silenced them.

Lucero's decision to document her mother's story gives a voice to both her mother and herself. Especially significant is Lucero's ability to give a voice and a place to her mother's story. Though Amada's husbands have prevented her from achieving an education and relaying her stories, Lucero can break free of the cultural restraints that often require Latinas to engage solely in the roles of mother and wife. In choosing to tell her family's stories, Lucero counters the epistemologies of her school. Lucero's storytelling also indicates the use of Rendón's sentipensante pedagogy, in which a balance is achieved through "inner work, focusing on emotional and spiritual nurturance, and outer work, involving service and action in the world" (135). Storytelling allows Lucero to reflect on her identity and positionality, inviting readers to engage in similar strategies, thereby balancing the focus on "inner" and "outer" work.

Lucero can also provide her perspective regarding her mother's and father's lives from this space. The combination of Lucero's story intertwined with her mother's and father's family histories allows Lucero's story to emerge from a third space. Lucero's ability to interrelate these various perspectives reveals that each is a part of her story. Lucero purposely places her story and herself within this in-between space to present her multiplicity; such tactics position her as a "strategic essentialist." Citing Irigaray, Emma Pérez refers to an individual who positions herself in this space as a "strategic essentialist," who is described as "one who exercises political representation, or identity politics, within hegemonic structures. The strategy asserts countersites within dominant society. As a dynamic process, this tactic gives voices to each new marginalized social or political group, bonded temporarily at specific historical moments" ("Irigaray's Female Symbolic" 87–88). Chicanas and Latinas residing in the United States employ strategic essentialism when they embrace their Chicana/Latina identity and reenvision it. Rather than contextualizing this identity solely within the racist and discriminatory experiences encountered, Latinas can reappropriate it. Significant is the site from which Chicanas and Latinas reappropriate and recontextualize their identity. This occurs often in the third space of education, where Chicanas and Latinas assert a specific politics of Chicana and Latina identity, including the epistemologies and identities of learning institutions and their cultural environments. Even more significant is that in the third space of education, Lucero attains agency in both worlds because she constantly integrates two types of knowledge. Agency is attained in the Anglocentric world through the mastery of the "tools" of education, such as reading and writing. Mastery of such tools also allows Lucero to engage in resistance. This rejection of binary thinking also signals a point of resistance and empowerment because she chooses to recreate her ways of thinking. Furthermore, Lucero engages in transformational resistance, as Daniel G. Solórzano and Dolores Delgado Bernal describe. Their description of the fourth form of resistance is fundamental and referred to as transformational.

This type of resistance "refers to student behavior that illustrates both a critique of oppression and a desire for social justice" (Solórzano and Bernal 319). I contend that Lucero engages in transformational resistance when she chooses to hear her family's and communities' stories and pass them on. In this way, Lucero participates in what Solórzano and Bernal refer to as "internal resistance" in which one "appears to conform to institutional or cultural norms and expectations, however individuals are consciously engaged in a critique of oppression" (324). Though it may appear that Lucero is conforming to society by continuing with her education, she does so with the express purpose of weaving the epistemologies learned there with those of her home, especially using storytelling.

Lucero can be described as a strategic essentialist because of the position from which she reveals her story. Her interweaving of her mother's stories with her father's and her own demonstrates her acceptance of these multiple identities. Within this context, Lucero employs strategic essentialism and becomes a strategic essentialist because she includes the stories of her mother, her father, and herself. She purposely presents these perspectives to assert a specific identity politics of mestizaje. This assertion is significant because she also presents it from a Chicana perspective, countering the dominant Anglo patriarchal society. This emergence of a countersite allows Lucero to give voice to her mother, father, Mexican immigrants, Tejanxs, and Chicanxs. She does not choose one dominant voice to represent the marginalized; instead, Lucero focuses on the often unheard story of the Mexican woman's border crossing and the challenges she must endure to earn a better education and future for her children. She also emphasizes the voice of the Tejanxs who occupied the land before the Anglos came and stole it. From this countersite, this third space, where Amada and Lucero place their story to contextualize their exploration of their mestizaje, thus renders this identity in a positive light.

As Lucero becomes more familiar with her family's stories, she questions her subjectivity and the dominant ideologies of U.S. school systems. Lucero's desire to contest the epistemologies of her school signals a significant shift in her consciousness. At this point, Lucero finally discovers the need to adopt a mestizaje of epistemologies, or rather, she understands that a balance of multiple epistemologies will allow her to embrace her identity. This understanding occurs once Lucero enters the Coatlicue state as a part of the path of conocimiento, which Anzaldúa describes as a point where you

> begin to know and accept the self uncovered by the trauma, you pull the blinders off, take in the new landscape in brief glances. Gradually you arouse the agent in this drama, begin to act, to dis-identify with the fear and the isolation. You sit quietly and meditate, trance into an altered state of consciousness, temporarily suspending your usual frames of reference and beliefs while your creative self seeks a solution to your problem by being receptive to new patterns of association. ("Now Let Us" 553)

Once Lucero has reached this state, she finally understands the importance of her family's stories. Lucero's fear is accompanied by the desire to hear such stories, as she explains that "a part of me doesn't want to hear it; it's just that her stories don't leave me alone, even when I wish they'd go back into the cupboard where Mami picks them out along with her spices" (González 133). Lucero's fear is also the realization that though she may not want to hear such stories about her family because they may cause grief, they must still be told. In deciding to share her family's stories, Lucero shifts into the crossing stage of the path of conocimiento, where action calls her out of the Coatlicue stage of depression and passive inaction. Thus, in choosing to write about and share her family's stories, Lucero "crosses" beyond Coatlicue, the stage of self-loathing and inaction, allowing her to engage in the next stage of questioning and reenvisioning her life experiences, which she begins to do as she learns more stories from her father's side of the family and considers how to share those narratives as they relate to her own experiences.

Lucero learns from her father that as "the eldest son, [he] was entrusted with top-secret for-your-eyes-only family stories, [and] says he has to give them to me, the firstborn daughter" (González 109). Though Lucero's father passes on the family stories, he also makes her promise that she will not share what he's told her with others because it would embarrass the family. However, to cope with who she is, Lucero must share her family's stories because they are also her story. Through storytelling, intertwining her story with those of her parents, Lucero can reflect on her identity and the multiple epistemologies she must juggle and sustain. Taking one's story out to the world is the next stage of the path of conocimiento, following the questioning of identity and positionality in society. Anzaldúa notes that in this storytelling stage, you choose "to compose a new history and self—to rewrite your autohistoria. You want to be transformed again; you want a keener mind, a stronger spirit, a wiser soul" ("Now Let Us" 559). This reflection is precisely what Lucero seeks to do in gathering the stories of her family as she comes to know them and herself better and better with each narrative. In hearing these stories alongside the knowledge obtained in the school environment, Lucero engages in a mestizaje of epistemologies, balancing the information she obtains from school with the knowledge gained from interacting with her mother, father, and aunts.

The exposure to storytelling further allows Lucero to critique her position in society while encouraging her to seek social justice. Solórzano and Bernal explain that transformational resistance in school emerges from "their roots and their own family and personal histories" (322). It is necessary to balance the family and personal histories of students with the formal knowledge they attain in school so that they may understand the significance of such information. The realization that such knowledge is just as necessary as formal schooling emerges as resistance because Latinx students understand that other types of knowledge are also legitimate. Formal schooling provides an avenue through which Latinas such as Lucero may continue to pass along such stories through writing and interaction with others. The sharing of such stories, engaging in counterstorytelling, is essential because it is "a technique of telling the story of those experiences that are often not told (i.e., those on the margins of society) and a tool for analyzing and challenging the stories of those in power and whose story is a natural part of the dominant discourse—the majoritarian story" (328). By engaging in such counterstorytelling, Lucero can help to build community within her own culture, challenge the dominance of one epistemology over others, and provide a way to understand and transform the education system and society.

Storytelling is also conveyed through the distinct types of dances Lucero's aunts attempt to teach her. Once again, the kitchen space in which these stories and knowledge are conveyed is essential. The kitchen is often the site of shared knowledge and stories that help to balance the Anglocentric histories and narratives Lucero encounters in the school system. Herrera notes that "the kitchen is also the site of female bonding and knowledge cultivated by Lucero's aunts—Amada's sisters—who provide their niece with humorous essential advice on how to navigate life, love, and men" (451). This knowledge is passed down through the stories they tell and their personalities, and primarily through the types of dances they attempt to teach Lucero. She explains each aunt's specialty: "Tía Toñia's man-eating rumbas. Cuca *la flaca* with her pinecone *chichis* and shriveled hips triple-stepping to the *cha-cha-chá*. Tía Paquita's *rico* mambo scaring the baby and making the dogs howl. My mother's fired-up polkas to get back at my father who doesn't dance. And the best for last, Lilia's *danzón*, which is a French waltz mixed with their slaves' revolting, she says, and look how much better it got" (González 99). As each aunt attempts to teach Lucero how to dance using her unique style, each tells the niece about her loves and stories. Sharing their stories allows Lucero's aunts to contest dominant Anglocentric ideology and bring their stories to light in the kitchen space while they style her hair and "beautify" her. As Herrera notes, in sharing this knowledge with Lucero, the kitchen becomes "an intimate site of intergenerational female bonding. No longer a passive 'place' designated for women, the kitchen as Chicana/Mexicana critical space grants the women mobility, freedom from men, and agency and autonomy modeled to their young daughter and niece" (451). This bonding experience becomes vital for a protagonist such as Lucero, who does not experience such sympathy and concern when at school. Thus, while at home with her family, Lucero gains essential knowledge to help her navigate the world as a woman and Mexican American, allowing her another kind of epistemology from which to shift beyond those taught in school. At the same time, while Lucero's aunts choose to convey their stories through the art of dance and oral storytelling, she continues to share those stories through the act of writing. Such dances and storytelling are significant because Lucero is a mestiza who represents multiple cultures and epistemologies. As Anzaldúa reveals, the act of writing allows mestizas such as Lucero to reconstruct her identity and her aunt's identities because she chooses to wield the pen as a "weapon and means of transformation" while also "reclaiming the agency of reinscribing, taking off their inscriptions and reinscribing ourselves, our own identities, our own cultures" (*Interviews* 189).

As Lucero listens to all her family stories, she begins to understand she can reconstruct her identity and resist Anglocentric epistemologies through storytelling. Paulo Freire explains, "To no longer be prey to its [oppression's] force, one must emerge from it and turn upon it. This can be done only utilizing the praxis: reflection and action upon the world to transform it" (51). As a Chicana, Lucero must not only reflect and act upon the world to transform it, but she must also develop what Anzaldúa refers to as a "mestiza consciousness," which allows for the breakdown of the "subject-object duality that keeps her a prisoner" and engagement in a "massive uprooting of dualistic thinking in the individual and collective consciousness" (*Borderlands* 102). In Lucero's case, she must achieve consciousness to break free of the dualistic knowledge she encounters at home and school. Instead, Lucero's awareness of the need to adopt a mestizaje of epistemologies, a mix of several types of knowledge, allows her to question the dominant ideologies of her school and society. Lucero's awareness also emerges from her mother's insistence on achieving a formal U.S. education while remembering who she is. Amada attempts to convey the importance of her daughter's culture and identity: "'Never forget you're a *mexicana*,' she says. 'With every breath you take, show them we're equal to them in every way. They think they're better, but we're all just the same, though your father believes their superior ideas he's heard all his life. They think we're savages, so show them. Show them, *mijita*'" (164). Amada's advice reveals her understanding that a mestizaje of epistemologies is necessary for her daughter and other children to survive. She acknowledges the need for a U.S. education while maintaining her identity and cultural epistemologies as a Mexican American woman.

Lucero's transformation and acceptance of a mestizaje of epistemologies is especially revealed in the novel's last scene. Lucero describes a bar full of dancing people from all over the world. Her mother, father, brothers, sisters, and grandparents are in the bar. Lucero takes special note of the various cultures and races present: "The *francés* is bragging that his town is where they make cognac, offering his hand to that woman wearing a Mexican *huipil*, impressed by *las doñas* and their black-shawled *sevillana*" (González 242). There is a bearded man named Osama from Dénia and a "Nefertiti-looking woman" from the African coast. All these people are dancing together, and they are all described as Lucero's family. The dance they are all engaging in is significant, a *polkita*, which is described as a mixture of many dances: yet another symbol of Lucero's mestiza identity and knowledge. Lucero finally realizes she is mestiza, a mix of many distinct cultures and types of expertise. She finally understands that her identity is fluid like a river and that she is never one identity all the time; instead, she has many different ones at various times. Accepting a mestizaje of epistemologies eventually allows Lucero to accept her histories, stories, and mestiza roots while balancing them with a U.S. education. Specifically, storytelling indicates Lucero's acceptance of a mestizaje of epistemologies because her story invites others to collectively reflect and resist oppressive binaries. Lucero's proficiency in English and writing allows her to convey her family's stories to remember, reinscribe, resist, and heal. Significant is the fact that Lucero's stories help her to heal the identity and communal splits that she has encountered. In this way, Lucero begins to accept her multiple selves while inviting her cultural community to join her in her educational journey.

This chapter has allowed me to critically examine a Chicana protagonist who not only encounters the education/educación conflict but adopts a mestizaje of epistemologies as a method of surviving and negotiating through this dilemma. In the following chapter, I explore the education/educación conflict as it is encountered and discussed in the testimonios of Latinas in K–12 and academia. I will demonstrate how the authors of such testimonios, like the protagonist of *Golondrina*, develop a theory of a mestizaje of epistemologies to negotiate their multiple identities and ways of knowing at home and school.

4

THE EDUCATION/EDUCACIÓN CONFLICT IN ACADEMIA

Reconciling Academic and Cultural Epistemologies in Latina Testimonios

In chapter three, I focused on revealing how the protagonist of *Golondrina, Why Did You Leave Me?* utilized and adopted a mestizaje of epistemologies to negotiate her institutional and cultural knowledge. I will continue to apply my theory of a mestizaje of epistemologies in this chapter as it pertains to Latinas' education testimonios and experiences in K–12 and academia, specifically their graduate school experiences. I explore testimonios and stories presented in *Telling to Live: Latina Feminist Testimonios*, *This Bridge Called My Back: Writings by Radical Women of Color*, and *This Bridge We Call Home: Radical Visions for Transformation* and the strategies that Latinas in academia have developed to negotiate their various cultural and institutional epistemologies and identities throughout time. I will discuss how the Latinas within these texts reach an awareness of their position between multiple epistemologies in the third space of education and develop survival strategies such as a mestizaje of epistemologies, which allows them to succeed in K–12 and academia yet retain ties to their cultural community. Though these texts were written twenty-plus years ago, I argue that they set the foundation for a better understanding of how the education landscape has changed throughout time for Latinas, how they have utilized methods such as a mestizaje of epistemologies in the past, and how they continue to use such strategies today as some of these same issues of racial and ethnic discrimination persist in the education system.

This Bridge Called My Back: Writings by Radical Women of Color, co-edited by Gloria E. Anzaldúa and Cherríe Moraga, is a collection of essays, poetry, stories, and testimonios written by feminists of color during the late 1970s and published in 1981. Through this collection, various women representing diverse Latina cultures discuss the intersectionality of feminism, the oppressions they have encountered as women of color, and the strategies they employ to negotiate those struggles. Though published over forty years ago, this text continues to be pivotal in understanding intersectional feminism in the past and today. Twenty years after the publication of *This Bridge Called My Back*, Gloria E. Anzaldúa and AnaLouise Keating returned to discussions of intersectional feminism via *This Bridge We Call Home: Radical Visions for Transformation*, published in 2002. Like the first anthology, the most recent edition gathers new contributions of essays, stories, poetry, and other narratives written by women of color as they contemplate how feminist consciousness has adapted in the twenty-first century. Similarly, *Telling to Live: Latina Feminist Testimonios*, published in 2001 by the Latina Feminist Group, continues along the same vein as the *Bridge* anthologies. However, the contributors of this collection utilize testimonios to share their journeys of identity exploration, especially as they encounter intersectional, sexist, oppressive systems in school and academia. Though these collections were written between twenty and fifty years ago, I argue that it is necessary to look at them and their testimonios to understand better the trajectory of the education/educación conflict experienced by Latinas and Chicanas throughout the decades. These narratives set the stage for the following chapter, in which I will compare education testimonios of the past with those of contemporary times, paying particular attention to the strategies employed by Latinas and Chicanas, such as a mestizaje of epistemologies, and how those have changed as education and academia undergo significant variations throughout time. I will also use the following chapter to discuss the continued significance of these texts, as evidenced by student testimonios and reactions, especially to the original *Bridge* anthology in my Women Authors course.

Exploring these testimonios allows me to demonstrate the complexity of the education/educación conflict by focusing on excerpts where Latinas discuss how they cope with their mixed identities and conflicting epistemologies of their cultures and learning institutions. I submit that these texts reveal how Latinas in the academy have resisted complete assimilation by sharing their stories and maintaining ties to their cultural communities, languages, and histories through the adoption of a mestizaje of epistemologies. Specifically, I will examine Gloria Anzaldúa's "Speaking in Tongues: A Letter to Third World Women Writers," Cherríe Moraga's "La Güera," Irene Lara's "Healing Sueños for Academia," Tatiana de la tierra's "Aliens and Others in Search of the Tribe in Academe," Celia Alvarez's "Snapshots from My Daze in School," and Liza Fiol-Matta's "Another Way to Grow Up Puerto Rican." I focus on these authors' experiences for numerous reasons. Each woman relays the oppressions she encountered in various educational settings because of the racism and sexism of teachers, fellow students, or the system of education itself. The problem of the education system becomes evident once a comparative analysis is made between it and Foucault's discussion of the figure of the ideal soldier, which I argue has striking similarities with the manipulation of the Latina student in the education system.

Foucault's discussion of discipline in the context of students' docile bodies begins with the soldier's malleable form. Foucault explains that the figure of the ideal soldier was at once recognizable due to specific markers such as strength, courage, and pride. However, to achieve the figure of the perfect soldier, it was discovered that the body must first become docile to those in control. Foucault argues that "a body is docile that may be subjected, used, transformed, and improved" (136). At this point, the body is discovered to be an "object and target of power" (136). The physical control of a soldier's body ensures that they can be manipulated and improved to maintain discipline throughout the ranks. Foucault describes the figure of the ideal soldier in the late eighteenth century as "something that can be made; out of a formless clay, an inapt body, the machine required can be constructed; posture is gradually corrected; a calculated constraint runs slowly through each part of the body, mastering it, making it pliable, ready at all times, turning silently into the automatism of habit" (135). The physical movements, attitude, and posture of the soldier's body are gradually manipulated, transformed, and improved through disciplinary methods.

Similarly, Latina students must also endure becoming the figure of the ideal student. Also important are those people exerting control not simply because they have power over another's body but because they can direct how things are operated, the techniques used, and the speed and efficiency with which they are conducted. This is all significant because the discipline of the body allows for quick and effective production. These disciplinary methods emerged in institutions such as prisons and hospitals and were gradually adopted by the military and school systems. Among schools and other institutions, "the meticulousness of the regulations, the fussiness of the inspections, the supervision of the smallest fragment of life and of the body will soon provide, in the context of the school, the barracks, the hospital or the workshop, a laicized content, an economic or technical rationality for this mystical calculus of the infinitesimal and the infinite" (Foucault 140). As used by the military, the slightest rules of discipline and punishment slowly begin to be used in contexts such as schools.

This understanding of the figure of the soldier as one that can be molded, manipulated, transformed, and improved through the docile body clarifies how assimilation and acculturation affect Latinx students. Foucault's theory of discipline's emergence from the docile soldier's body helps explain how alienation emerges from disciplining the Latinx student's body and mind and why this is especially important to understanding school success for this particular group.

I utilize these testimonios to demonstrate how each Latina author encounters the experience of being manipulated into the "figure of the ideal student," for which U.S. institutions of learning require a docile body and mind. Especially prevalent is the concept of docile minds because the Anglocentric assimilation and racism of institutions of learning exert forceful control of Latinas' bodies and minds through problematic curriculum and pedagogies and systemic racism.

RESISTING BINARIES THROUGH A MESTIZAJE OF EPISTEMOLOGIES IN LATINA TESTIMONIOS

Assimilation and the systemic racism of the education system allow schools and society to maintain a certain amount of control over Latina bodies and minds. Such power is further exerted by the U.S. education system using binary oppositions, as mentioned in chapter 2. Binaries such as male/female, Anglo/Latina, upper class / working class, individual/collective, and heterosexual/queer are established not only by the U.S. education system but by the Anglo upper-class heterosexual patriarchy. The problem with such binaries lies in the connotations associated with each "side" of the binary system.

I argue that each woman's encounter, as described via the following testimonios, with such oppressions and her awareness of them propel her into the third space of education, where she learns how to negotiate between academia and her cultural community, rejecting the binary system that insists all or most of her identity markers are negative. Such experiences become significant because, in each case, the writer learns how to balance her life and ways of knowing in academia with her cultural identity; in this way, these Latina writers also show that they reject individualism for the communal. Feminist scholar Lorgia García Peña emphasizes the importance of community in her text *Community as Rebellion: A Syllabus for Surviving Academia as Women of Color*; she argues:

> To be in the university as women of color, as women from colonized nations, as migrants is to be in tension with ourselves. It is a position of discomfort. To be in academia and remain *una dura* [a strong woman], we need to be comfortable existing within discomfort, never aiming to belong or conform, for conformity is another form of death. To conform to academia is to renounce our collective project of being and belonging. Our strategy, therefore, must be to find ways to return to the discomfort through a feminist praxis of being, knowing, and doing. (56)

Peña, like many other Latina academics and scholars, notes that academia is not a welcoming space for women of color because it was not built for women of color, and thus, one might encounter discomfort in many ways, especially I argue through the education/educación conflict. The education/educación conflict is more than a fear of alienation from one's cultural community. It is also this fear of being unable to take one's family and cultural community along as they embark on the education journey. The way the authors of each work weave between cultural and academic epistemologies begins with their testimonando, or the act of testifying about their education experiences, and the product, which is the testimonios themselves.

Of particular importance is where and why these writings emerge. Each of these anthologies provides an introduction, a preface, or a foreword that explains the objective of the collection of stories and experiences. The 1981 introduction by Cherríe Moraga and Gloria Anzaldúa to *This Bridge Called My Back* asserts that the purpose of the text will be to reach students in learning institutions and women in diverse communities. This text aims to share the experiences of encountering and overcoming oppressions, such as sexism and racism, with other women and men who may or may not have met similar situations. Such sharing enables the writers and readers of the text to engage in healing and resistance together, thus forming a community and kinship. Moraga and Anzaldúa explain that they hope that this text may become a "revolutionary tool falling into the hands of people of all colors. Just as we have been radicalized in the process of compiling this book, we hope it will radicalize others into action" (lvi). Especially significant are the poems, stories, and experiences that focus on oppression encountered in schools. The authors' ability to write about such experiences and share them with others allows them to heal, become empowered, and engage in resistance. Such healing, empowerment, and resistance emerged most recently in my Women Authors course, a class focused on multiethnic women's literature and feminist theories. Over time, as our class engaged in further discussions of women's oppression within various institutions and academia, students found themselves more willing to share their own experiences of oppression, especially as we read *This Bridge Called My Back*. From these readings, a community of women scholars/readers/students emerged alongside a deep-seated kinship. Melanie K. Yazzie defines the notion of kin and kinship as one rooted in Indigenous relationships to place. However, Yazzie utilizes the term "in the abolitionist and decolonial sense to suggest something creative and future-oriented; the desire to build a world structured by relations of care, love, and abundance instead of relations of abandonment, harm, and scarcity" (1–2). This notion of kinship can emerge once readers are introduced to the various experiences of women of color within academia and the survival strategies they employ to navigate it.

Specifically, the stories, poems, and experiences in *This Bridge We Call Home* examine how women of color negotiate their multiple and complex identities and epistemologies. In the preface to *This Bridge We Call Home*, Gloria Anzaldúa indicates that the purpose in creating this anthology is partially due to the need to "continue the dialogue, rethink the old ideas, and germinate new theories." She continues, "In these pages we move from focusing on what has been done to us (victimhood) to a more extensive level of agency, one that questions what we're doing to each other, those in distant countries, and the earth's environment" ("(Un)natural Bridges" 2). Anzaldúa notes that continuing the dialogue begun in *This Bridge Called My Back* is necessary because the issues of oppression, racism, and sexism are more complex than initially thought. Especially significant is the fact that the education/educación conflict presented in *This Bridge Called My*

Back continues to persist and has seemingly become more complex in the intervening years, as some of the experiences revealed in *This Bridge We Call Home* attest.

Like the experiences portrayed in *This Bridge We Call Home*, many of the education testimonios in *Telling to Live* provide an understanding of how a mestizaje of epistemologies is adopted as a survival strategy by Latinas in academia to cope with the education/educación conflict. *Telling to Live* is markedly different from *This Bridge* anthologies because of the collaborative efforts of the writers, who refer to themselves as the Latina Feminist Group. The writers explain that "we began through a collective process and have sustained that commitment and collaboration throughout" to create a comfortable space where everyone could share their experiences freely (xi). The Latina Feminist Group further explains that the purpose of gathering to compose this anthology was to examine the differences and similarities of Latina feminists in higher education. Crucial is the authors' assertion that "because of our professional choices—to research, think, and write about Latinas in ways that take the subject seriously—we become marginalized by institutional cultures that reproduce hegemonic relations of power. With so few Latinas in higher education and intensifying workloads, we are caught between multiple constituencies, needs, and institutional demands" (8). Such marginalization also includes struggling to overcome the education/educación conflict, which positions Latinas between oppositional epistemologies and identities. However, the Latina Feminist Group's consciousness of the education/educación conflict, as exhibited through members' awareness of being caught between multiple epistemologies, is the first step toward achieving a mestizaje of epistemologies. Awareness of their position between multiple ideologies shifts many of the women of the Latina Feminist Group into the third space of education, where they adopt a mestizaje of epistemologies to survive and succeed in academia while retaining ties to their cultural knowledge and identities.

I examine testimonios in which Latinas become aware of an education/educación identity conflict, which becomes more complex as they work through academia. The reasons for expanding my analysis beyond Latina fictional literature to testimonios lie in the definition of the term *testimonio* itself. John Beverley's discussion of testimonio broadly defines it as "autobiography, autobiographical novel, oral history, memoir, confession, diary, interview, eyewitness report, life-history" (93). I would also add that the education testimonios of *Telling to Live*, examined in this chapter, should be included within the testimonio genre because of the aforementioned definition, though they may sometimes take the form of creative nonfiction works. In addition, Beverley asserts that testimonio-like texts often represent marginalized peoples such as "the 'native,' the woman, the insane, the criminal, the proletarian" (93). For my purposes here, I utilize all these definitions, including Beverley's explanation that testimonio "represents an affirmation of the individual subject, even of individual growth and transformation, but in connection with a group or class situation marked by marginalization, oppression, and struggle" (103). In the case of the three anthologies explored in this chapter, I argue that the education/educación conflict impels Latinas to tell and write their education testimonios, a vital part of attaining consciousness as part of a mestizaje of epistemologies. While most of the testimonios in *Telling to Live*, *This Bridge We Call Our Back*, and *This Bridge We Call Home* focus on the diverse experiences Latinas have encountered throughout the years, many also emphasize the similar oppressions Latinas have encountered in school, particularly K–12, and academia.[1] Despite the similarities shared by Latinas, emphasis on their diverse ethnic backgrounds, including Puerto Rican American, Cuban American, and Chicana, self-identifications are significant. To avoid monolithic assumptions, highlighting the diversity of these Latinas' experiences is necessary. In choosing to relay their shared experiences of oppression in the U.S. school system and their differences, these Latina authors hope to establish connections with other women who have experienced similar situations. These connections are vital to a mestizaje of epistemologies because they ensure the rejection of the individual/collective binary while also creating a new space, a new way of conceptualizing the world that invites each Latina's community to join her and vice versa. At the same time, I will note with my analyses that each scholar creates a specific site for herself and her community within the third space of education where they can simultaneously succeed, retain their cultural ties, and rebel.

---

1. In addition to the texts mentioned above, new anthologies attempt to tackle the oppressions women faculty of color continue to endure in academia: *Presumed Incompetent: The Intersections of Race and Class for Women in Academia*, by Gabriella Gutiérrez y Muhs, Yolanda Flores Niemann, Carmen G. González, and Angela P. Harris, which also now has a second volume.

THE EDUCATION/EDUCACIÓN CONFLICT IN LATINA TESTIMONIOS

An analysis of the education testimonios in *This Bridge Called My Back, This Bridge We Call Home,* and *Telling to Live* reveals the existence in the authors' lives of similar experiences and themes that include the education/educación conflict as it pertains to oppositional epistemologies and therefore identities, language, privilege, racism, classism, sexism, and stereotypes. The first shared experience is the education/educación conflict itself. Each Latina encounters the education/educación conflict once the ideologies of her family culture come into opposition with an institutional epistemology. This conflict is especially problematic because it may lead to contrasting identities. Each theory of knowing is associated with a specific cultural or school identity. If one epistemology is denied or favored over another, the same thing may occur regarding identity. Latinas often encounter educational and cultural social groups that require them to shift social identities. However, many Latinas encounter the dilemma of obtaining degrees while struggling to retain ties to their communities, as revealed in research by Aída Hurtado. She asks critical questions in her study of Chicanas who attain college degrees: "As my respondents obtain degrees, get hired in prestigious jobs, and no longer struggle economically, will they stop relating to their parents' struggles or... will they use their newfound success and professional privileges to help others like them advance as well?" (220). In addition, as Latinas obtain higher education degrees, there is a concern that their cultural ways of knowing may be lost.

Second, this conflict manifests itself when each Latina decides to maintain their home language, most often Spanish, or master the English language, thereby ensuring their success in school and society. It is especially problematic because English is usually privileged over Spanish in learning institutions. Third, each woman also acknowledges how privilege may or may not help to maintain or sever ties between herself and her culture. Fourth, each Latina describes experiences of racism, classism, or sexism once they are introduced into institutions of learning. Fifth, conflict is encountered as each woman attempts to fight the stereotypes often placed on them by educational institutions.

Resistance to this conflict emerges through telling and sharing these education testimonios. Acknowledging the education/educación conflict enables each woman to reinscribe her story into history, especially regarding education. Emma Pérez's exploration of Chicana history points out that we must focus on women's stories and histories that have long been ignored. Specifically, Pérez focuses on the activities and words of Chicanas, Mexicanas, indigenous women, and mestizas as they "intervene to do what [she calls] sexing the colonial imaginary, historically tracking women's agency on the colonial landscape" (*Decolonial Imaginary* 7). Focusing on the Latina experience allows the decolonizing history to begin, allowing room for those silenced to speak. Therefore, anthologies written by Latinas and women of color may bring their stories to the forefront. The essays that I examine shift the education testimonios of Latinas from the margins of history and literature to the center as they become objects of study.

Focusing on Latina histories and stories contests binary systems and the negative associations accompanying them. The exploration of each woman's education experiences thus reveals how being female, Latina, working-class, and queer need not be strictly associated with oppression. Instead, readers begin to understand that these identity markers are viewed as abnormal because they are considered threats by a patriarchal, Anglo, upper-class, and heterosexual culture—or the perceived norm.

REACHING AWARENESS IN THE THIRD SPACE OF EDUCATION

Not only do authors describe their experiences with the education/educación conflict, but such awareness also propels each author into the third space of education, as discussed in chapter 2. Each woman shifts into the third space because they recognize that they cannot truly belong to the first space, in which the epistemology of their culture dominates their life, nor can they comfortably reside in the second space, to which they are introduced through institutions of learning. Instead, there is a desire to hold on to the cultural teachings of their homes while demonstrating their intellectual abilities in learning institutions. Therefore, the Latina authors shift into the third space of education, where they weave between the spaces of institutional learning and cultural ways of knowing.

Such weaving strategies enact Chela Sandoval's concept of differential consciousness, previously defined in chapter 2. Though Sandoval begins her discussion of differential consciousness by placing it in the historical context of the Chicana feminist movement, I adapt her concept to apply it to Chicana education and literature. Sandoval explains that though women of color expressed a dislike for the white feminist movement's practices, they also learned how to involve themselves with it at specific points, but rarely for long. Sandoval further notes that although U.S. feminists of color worked within the white women's liberation movement, women of color rarely fully adopted the belief systems and identity politics of white feminists. Sandoval describes this activity using what Anzaldúa refers to as weaving "between and among" oppositional ideologies in a new space where the fifth mode of oppositional consciousness and activity is discovered (*Methodology* 57). However, Sandoval refers to this activity of consciousness as the "differential" because it allows an interweaving between multiple, often oppositional, ideological positionings. The purpose of enacting differential consciousness is to attain agency to "enlist and secure influence" (57). Thus, U.S. women of color can use differential consciousness to weave between multiple ideologies as a survival strategy in various situations.

Similarly, I argue that the writers of each essay—Alvarez, Anzaldúa, Moraga, Fiol-Matta, de la tierra, and Lara—describe the experience of weaving between multiple epistemologies, namely those of their culture and school/academia. In addition to shifting between multiple feminist movements, I assert that the female authors of these essays move between oppositional ideological positions as they pertain to academic and cultural epistemologies. In other words, once in the third space of education, Latinas understand the need to utilize particular epistemologies at school and home, neither ultimately succumbing to one or the other nor engaging in the privileging of one over another. Such shifting between epistemologies ensures survival and success at school and in their culture.

In each case, the authors describe moments in which they experience the education/educación conflict. Anzaldúa explains that she questioned the epistemologies of her home and her Mexican American identity when she was faced with writing in English. Though she drafts her poems in Spanish and English, Anzaldúa still feels "the rip-off of my native tongue" ("Speaking" 184). Similarly, Moraga realizes she has internalized the racism that Anglo culture has instilled within her: "I have had to confront the fact that much of what I value about being Chicana, about my family, has been subverted by Anglo culture and my cooperation with it" (28). While Anzaldúa and Moraga discuss the distancing they felt as they progressed through school, de la tierra and Lara explain how this problem becomes more pronounced in college and graduate school. Both women describe the pain of being unable to identify their cultures in their college classes and often submitting to silence for fear of failure.

Alvarez and Fiol-Matta also describe their experiences negotiating between multiple identities and the epistemologies of their culture and school. Alvarez explains that once in graduate school, she "constantly had to fight off their [her department's] stereotypical conceptions of my cultural and academic identity" (181). At the same time, Fiol-Matta notes, "It became obvious that, for my own survival, I needed to choose between being American and being Puerto Rican" (195). Each author's ability to recognize her experience with the education/educación conflict allows her the opportunity to reflect on the separation that often occurred between her school and cultural epistemologies and identities. Alvarez's and Fiol-Matta's unique positions as Latinas in predominantly white institutions force them to shift to the third space of education, where they question the institutional epistemologies; in short, they learn how to rebel. Their inability to completely accept the epistemologies of school and vice versa forces Alvarez and Fiol-Matta into an in-between space where they learn how to meld cultural and institutional ways of knowing together. Their ability to speak about such encounters signals a shift into the third space of education, where they can confront this conflict and eventually resist it through a mestizaje of epistemologies.

"SPEAKING IN TONGUES: A LETTER TO THE THIRD WORLD" AND THE EDUCATION/EDUCACIÓN CONFLICT

Part of the experience of the education/educación conflict includes the struggle to retain one's cultural language despite the English-only policies of institutions of learning and academia. Throughout *This Bridge Called My Back*, *This Bridge We Call Home*, and *Telling to Live*, various authors discuss the challenge of retaining ties to their culture as they progress through higher education and academia. One of the critical issues associated with the education/educación conflict—maintaining one's cultural language while also mastering the English language—is discussed in Anzaldúa's "Speaking in Tongues: A Letter to Third World Women Writers," Moraga's "La Güera," Alvarez's "Snapshots from My Daze in School," and Fiol-Matta's "Another Way to Grow Up Puerto Rican."

Though Anzaldúa, Moraga, Alvarez, and Fiol-Matta each discuss how language contributes to the education/educación conflict, it is essential to note that each experience is also quite different from the next and, therefore, not homogeneous. The similarities emerge through the sense of alienation each woman experiences because of a rejection of her cultural language in the school setting. Anzaldúa's "Speaking in Tongues: A Letter to Third World Women Writers," published in the original *Bridge* anthology, utilizes the letter format to call on women of color to write and theorize about their own lives experienced by writing from the body.

Anzaldúa explains, "Because white eyes do not want to know us, they do not bother to learn our language, the language which reflects us, our culture, our spirit. The schools we attended or didn't attend did not give us the skills for writing nor the confidence that we were correct in using our class and ethnic languages" ("Speaking" 184). In describing the discrimination Anzaldúa faced during her time in school, she explains the pain she felt in not being able to utilize her ethnic language at school. In sharing this experience, Anzaldúa calls on others to also share their experiences of discrimination. As Kia S. Rideaux explains, "Anzaldúa dared women of color to reawaken their unruly tongues through speeches, protests, writings, poems, drawings, songs, and any other forms of dissent . . . She pleaded that their voices no longer remain hidden or silent in regard to their own realities" (222). Through the sharing of her story, Anzaldúa calls out the education/educación conflict as part of the more considerable systemic racism of the education system that sought to silence and erase her home/cultural language. However, rather than remain silenced, Anzaldúa uses writing to share her pain while calling others to do the same. At this point in the letter, she acknowledges and calls out the education/educación conflict, while calling for a mestizaje of epistemologies as a strategy she can use through the composition and sharing of her education testimonio and narratives. Anzaldúa's use of a mestizaje of epistemologies emerges as she acknowledges, "I, for one, became adept at, and majored in English to spite, to show up, the arrogant racist teachers who thought all Chicano children were dumb and dirty. And Spanish was not taught in grade school. And Spanish was not required in High School. And though now I write my poems in Spanish and English I feel the rip-off of my native tongue" ("Speaking" 184). Anzaldúa's decision to major in English to oppose racist school systems and teachers demonstrates her ability to navigate the Anglocentric education system. However, she also points out that she refuses to completely assimilate, by writing her poetry in English and Spanish. Thus, she strategically chooses to assimilate to an extent by learning the English language and becoming proficient in it by majoring in this discipline while also retaining ties to her culture by refusing to forget her home language, Spanish.

Anzaldúa further achieves awareness of her position between multiple epistemologies as she begins the composition of her letter, "Speaking in Tongues: A Letter to Third World Women Writers." The composition starts with her reflection on the writing process and the struggle women of color must overcome to engage in writing. As Anzaldúa contemplates the importance of writing for women of color, she notes that there was and is a fear in writing because schools and teachers have rarely affirmed such skills in Chicanx students. Anzaldúa asserts that her culture and language were considered insignificant by her teachers and school, which served as a stimulus for her to counter the racist teachers by majoring in and becoming quite proficient in English. Anzaldúa's immediate reaction to the racism she experiences in school is to show those teachers that she can fully utilize and become an expert in the English language. However, this determination to spite the racist teachers who believed Chicanxs were dumb eventually comes back to haunt Anzaldúa once she realizes that she continues to feel a lack of connection to her native tongue. Though she demonstrates an English proficiency, her Spanish is almost completely lost in the process. The result of this erasure of her native language is a sense of loss and confusion of identity, resulting from the education/educación conflict.

In response to this conflict, Anzaldúa uses writing and the language of her home and school to contemplate her identity. Rather than forgo her cultural identity and the ways of thinking accompanying it, as represented by the Spanish language, Anzaldúa decides to use it when she communicates while also discussing its importance. Anzaldúa also utilizes the writing skills taught in school to discuss the importance of her culture, language, and identity.

Instead of ultimately succumbing to assimilation, Anzaldúa attempts to revive her native language and culture by authoring her poems in Spanish and English. She and others use writing, the tool that Anglos insisted she could not master, to "record what others erase when I speak, to rewrite the stories others have miswritten about me, about you... to show that I *can* and that I *will* write, never mind their admonitions to the contrary. And I will write about the unmentionables, never mind the outraged gasp of the censor and the audience" ("Speaking" 187). Anzaldúa's decision to utilize writing as a weapon to reinscribe her voice and story into history emerges as a survival strategy. Further, Anzaldúa's use of writing in the Spanish and English languages allows her to identify the oppressions she and others have encountered, especially in the school environment. Such acknowledgment and the method she chooses to reveal these oppressions indicate an adoption of a mestizaje of epistemologies. Anzaldúa consciously chooses to remember who she is through her writing and the languages she composes, which is evidence of a delicate balance between the epistemologies of the Anglocentric schools and her Chicana home. This new mestiza consciousness further encourages Anzaldúa to accept that her identity is constantly shifting and evolving.

CHERRÍE MORAGA'S "LA GÜERA" AND THE EDUCATION/EDUCACIÓN CONFLICT

Similarly, Moraga realizes that she has long engaged in silencing her family's voices and her culture by disowning the language she knew best, "ignor[ing] the words and rhythms that were the closest to me. The sounds of my mother and aunts gossiping—half in English, half in Spanish—while drinking cerveza in the kitchen" (29). Like Anzaldúa, Moraga utilizes her writing, via "La Güera," with the realization that she has long suppressed the Spanish language of her home, thereby denying a part of herself.

Though Anzaldúa and Moraga admit to silencing their cultural languages, the awareness of this occurrence also brings to light their part in accepting the binary thought process of U.S. schools and society. This reflection further indicates an achievement of a mestiza consciousness. Awareness is propelled by a traumatic experience, such as the acknowledgment that their language has been stripped from them. Anzaldúa and Moraga acknowledge that they allowed the silencing of their native language, primarily through privileging the English language. However, each woman's attempts to reclaim the Spanish language and openly discuss her reflections on this matter reveal her decision to reject binary thinking and adopt a new way of thinking, a mestizaje of epistemologies, a blending and shifting of home and school knowledge.

Another aspect of the education/educación conflict includes the role that privilege plays. In "La Güera," Moraga begins by noting the privilege she held because she is light skinned and well educated; she observes:

> I was educated and wore it with a keen sense of pride and satisfaction, my head propped up with the knowledge, from my mother, that my life would be easier than hers. I was educated; but more than this, I was "la Güera": fair skinned.

Born with the features of my Chicana mother, but the skin of my Anglo father, I had it made. (25)

Though Moraga admits that growing up she experienced this privilege and was quite proud of it, she also observed that she had "no choice but to enter into the life of my mother" (25). When Moraga finally decides to admit she is a lesbian she also begins to identify with her mother's oppression as a poor, uneducated Chicana.

Like Anzaldúa, Moraga also becomes "anglocized" ("La Güera" 25) because her mother desired to protect her children and ensure that they could pass in the white world. In a letter to Barbara Smith, she writes that as a poet, "I denied the voice of my brown mother—the brown in me. I have acclimated to the sound of a white language" (29). It is at this point that Moraga confronts her education/educación conflict because she finally realizes that she has denied a part of herself simply because she could pass as an Anglo woman. However, as scholar Cynthia Cruz points out, Moraga's "interrogations of her identity as lesbian lends itself to the possibilities of solidarity with women whose positions differ drastically from her own" (47). Cruz notes that for Cherríe Moraga, "reclamation begins with the body that houses multiple identities. Each component of the brown body has its own story to tell—the lesbian mouth, the bent back in the fields, the dismembered daughter—and its deconstruction is a necessary process of reclaiming and re-imagining the histories and forms of agencies of women who are unrepresented and unheard" (48). Through the acknowledgment of the privilege afforded to her because of her light skin and her acceptance of her lesbian self, Moraga begins to accept her multiple selves and ways of knowing the world: what it means to be a woman of color, a woman of working-class status, and a woman who has often been subjected to silence as her mother has. Connected to such realizations is the understanding that Moraga must acknowledge how privilege has shifted her away from the epistemologies of her culture and mother. Moraga also concedes that she lacks certain privileges, especially once she embraces her lesbian identity. Thus, privilege and identity reveal themselves as more complex than previously thought. However, acknowledgment of certain privileges shifts Moraga into the third space of education, where she begins to contemplate her multiple identities associated with her mother as a working-class woman of color and her own identity as a lesbian Chicana.

Similarly, Moraga achieves awareness of the education/educación conflict once she reflects on her identity and history. Moraga contemplates, "What is my responsibility to my roots—both white and brown, Spanish-speaking and English? I am a woman with a foot in both worlds; and I refuse the split. I feel the necessity for dialogue. Sometimes I feel it urgently" (32). As with Anzaldúa, Moraga's consciousness of this split identity shifts her into the third space of education. There, she contemplates her multiple identities and epistemologies while also deciding to balance her cultural and institutional epistemologies. More importantly, Moraga understands that she cannot forsake one aspect of her identity for the other. Moraga notes that one epistemology cannot take precedence over another. This realization leads Moraga to question the values and privileges she and others have engaged in because "we are afraid to see how we have taken the values of our oppressor into our hearts and turned them against ourselves and one another" (30). However, Moraga's ability to recognize the oppressor/oppressed within herself and share this revelation with others indicates an adoption of a mestizaje of epistemologies.

Like Anzaldúa, Moraga utilizes writing to share the conflict of identity she has experienced because of exposure to Anglocentric institutions of learning and society. This mestizaje of epistemologies arises when Moraga engages in a differential consciousness within the contexts of her identity and education. Rather than choosing between her white and brown selves and her Spanish-speaking and English-speaking selves, she decides to weave together multiple identities and epistemologies. Moraga engages in a mestizaje of epistemology by remembering her experiences, noting her privilege, remembering her family's stories, and writing about them.

CELIA ALVAREZ'S "SNAPSHOTS FROM MY DAZE IN SCHOOL" AND LIZA FIOL-MATTA'S "ANOTHER WAY TO GROW UP PUERTO RICAN"

Alvarez's and Fiol-Matta's experiences differ slightly from Anzaldúa's and Moraga's because the former admit the ease with which they engage in bilingual education. However, like Anzaldúa and Moraga, Alvarez begins her story by explaining that her bilingual abilities are the tools she used to negotiate through the education/educación conflict she encountered in the private schools of her youth. Alvarez explains,

I learned Spanish at home, from my mother and grandparents, during my early childhood years. I later sustained and developed my Spanish language abilities through my meditating role as a translator for my mother and numerous others in the neighborhood. My mother, a cultural nationalist in her own right, insisted we speak Spanish at the home, even as adults. She explicitly affirmed our Puerto Rican identity within the confines of the United States. Thanks to my mother, I am bilingual today. My father, who was in daily contact with "mainstream" society through work, brought English home. Fortunately, I had acquired both languages by the time I went to school. (179)

Despite the awareness of multiple cultures brought about by her bilingual abilities, Alvarez also notes that she felt a need to "reconcile the privileges and isolation of an excellent academic formation with the other sites of myself as a second-generation, bilingual, working-class, New York–born, Puerto Rican woman" (179). Although Alvarez can transition "smoothly" into her education because of her ability to speak English, she acknowledges that this ability also marked her as "different" in her cultural and academic communities. Like Anzaldúa and Moraga, Alvarez acknowledges her part in the binary thought process, revealing how it has disconnected her from her family and culture. However, recognizing this fact allows Alvarez to rectify this dilemma by accepting her multiple identities, including being an educated, working-class *puertorriqueña* (Puerto Rican woman).

Like Alvarez, Fiol-Matta can also transition smoothly into her education because she grew up in an army family where she often moved from place to place. As a result of the multiple moves and encounters with various cultures, she learned how to juggle identities, cultures, and languages. Especially significant is Fiol-Matta's ability to speak "perfectly enunciated English" while at the homes of her friends and understanding the Spanish that was often spoken "at home, as in so many Puerto Rican families in the armed forces" (193). However, such negotiation between her culture's and school's languages becomes complicated in cities such as Colorado Springs, where Fiol-Matta discovers that "the better my English, the better my relationship with my teachers," and in Columbia, South Carolina, where she realizes "the better I memorized lines from my reader, the greater distance from my mother" (193). Fiol-Matta's understanding of the English language eventually leads to an easy transition and success in school; however, she also notes that other consequences include separation from her mother and her culture.

Fiol-Matta's education/educación conflict becomes further complicated when her family returns to Puerto Rico. It is there that her easy assimilation into U.S. culture and language truly becomes problematic. In Puerto Rico, the separation between Fiol-Matta and her family's culture and language becomes evident. As she explains, "I stumbled through Spanish with Abuela and my mother's sisters" (194). Because Fiol-Matta inadvertently privileges the English language to pass as an American and succeed in school, she forsakes the Spanish of her family. Not until Spanish becomes necessary to communicate does Fiol-Matta realize its importance.

In each case, Anzaldúa, Moraga, Alvarez, and Fiol-Matta realize the importance of the Spanish language while noting that this is not a view held by most schools. Each woman's experience reveals that the inability to utilize English often leads to alienation from peers, teachers, and the school. Each woman also notes the significance of mastering the English language regarding their academic success. In contrast, the use of the Spanish language is rarely encouraged or validated, thereby suggesting that each woman's culture and Latina identity has also been deemed a hindrance. Although the women who successfully master bilingualism discuss their "smooth" transitions to U.S. schools, they also point out the conflicts they encounter despite such knowledge. Dolores Delgado Bernal's 2002 study of students and bilingualism reveals that "most of them [students] felt that their bilingualism had a positive impact on them academically and socially. They seemed to draw strength from using both Spanish and English in academic and social settings. A few students also spoke passionately about their bilingualism in terms of identity and the importance of maintaining their home language" ("Critical Race Theory" 114). This study demonstrates how detrimental the education/educación conflict can be if one's home language is eradicated from the school curriculum. Bernal points to the importance of bilingualism in shaping and affirming multiple identities and epistemologies. Despite this study, experiences such as Fiol-Matta's and Alvarez's also reveal how the education/educación conflict can still emerge despite students being bilingual.[2]

---

2. Though Fiol-Matta and Alvarez for the most part had positive encounters due to bilingualism, it is important to note the recent immigration laws enacted in the last decades in states such as Arizona and Alabama in response to immigration from Mexico to the United States. Laws such as HB 2281, banning ethnic studies programs, also including the banning of English language learning programs to eliminate the cultural identities of Mexican immigrant popula-

Similarly, Alvarez and Fiol-Matta recognize they were persecuted in school because of their identities as Latinas while also noting the distance that education has created between themselves and their families. Alvarez explains the pain of not being able to share with her mother the alienation felt at school as fellow students challenge her presence. Fiol-Matta also recognizes the discomfort when she returns to Puerto Rico and is unable to clearly articulate in Spanish while also realizing that assimilation was easy because she did not "seem Puerto Rican to them" (194). These realizations allow Alvarez and Fiol-Matta to adopt a mestizaje of epistemologies as evidenced through Alvarez's decision to "cross the borders between race, class, and gender" and Fiol-Matta's decision to choose "against my father," a Puerto Rican U.S. Army officer (195).

Though each woman describes the alienation she experiences from her cultural identity, school, or family, each woman's ability to recognize such alienation is crucial to resolving the education/educación conflict. This step shifts them into the third space of education, where they decide to adopt a mestizaje of epistemologies, as revealed through their decisions to begin accepting their multiple selves and epistemologies.

Specifically, Alvarez balances her multiple selves and identities by utilizing her academic skills to help her cultural community. Despite this conscious decision to adopt a mestizaje of epistemologies, Alvarez notes the complexity of attempting this feat. She notes the following questions continue to plague her: "What price have I paid for my 1954 birthright to an equal education? What marks of institutional abuse in my body after all these years? Why is it that even after mastering the ivy nuances of the academy, I am not heard?" (184). Alvarez points out that though she has "succeeded" in academia by achieving tenure and balancing that with working in and for her community, the struggle continues.

Fiol-Matta also notes the complexity of balancing her cultural and academic epistemologies and identities. Fiol-Matta's decision to become "immersed in the literature of Black Power and Young Lords movements in the United States" signals a shift away from her father (195). Though she consciously chooses to maintain a balance between her multiple selves and

---

tion here in the United States. Anne-Marie Nuñez and Elizabeth Murakami-Ramalho note that "dual-language K–12 programs are effective in helping English learning (EL) students—defined as students who do not speak English well enough yet to be considered proficient—to learn languages and to improve in broader content areas such as math" (2).

epistemologies, the decision is not so easy because her father remains a part of the U.S. Army, a symbol of Anglocentric assimilation. Fiol-Matta's decision to refuse complete assimilation is crucial in understanding the adoption of a mestizaje of epistemologies because it demonstrates that the culture of institutional environments does not always embrace a choice such as the one she has made. In choosing to embrace her cultural identity, yet doing so because she had once accepted assimilation, Fiol-Matta begins to weave together multiple epistemologies.

ACKNOWLEDGING PRIVILEGE IN TATIANA DE LA TIERRA'S "ALIENS AND OTHERS IN SEARCH OF THE TRIBE IN ACADEME" AND RETAINING TIES TO CULTURE IN IRENE LARA'S "HEALING SUEÑOS FOR ACADEMIA"

Just as Moraga, Alvarez, and Fiol-Matta discuss the privileges afforded to them in learning how to negotiate academia, de la tierra discusses the privilege she has because of her light skin in "Aliens and Others in Search of the Tribe in Academe." De la tierra explains that though she classifies herself as Latina and therefore expects to be classified as the "Other," she must also acknowledge that "as a light-skinned person I have white privilege. Also, I do not have a Spanish accent when I speak in English now, while my mother does, and my father doesn't even speak English" (359). By acknowledging the privilege she has because of her light skin and ability to speak accentless English, de la tierra also points to the separation between herself, her family, and her culture.

De la tierra, like Moraga, acknowledges the privilege she has due to her accentless English and light skin, coupled with the revelation that she is a Chicana lesbian, which leads to greater awareness of her position between multiple epistemologies. De la tierra notes that though she can pass as Anglo, she does not identify with "white culture or politics" and instead identifies as a "woman of color" (359). Despite the ability to pass, de la tierra consciously chooses to identify herself as a woman of color, especially once in graduate school, having struggled to discover herself in the literature of her courses. However, such experiences help de la tierra to acknowledge the education/educación conflict encountered in school, while also affirming and strengthening her identity as a Chicana lesbian. The affirmation of her identities further signals a break from the harmful methodologies of binary thinking.

In addition to recognizing the invalidation of cultural languages, privilege, and internal racism, Lara, de la tierra, and Alvarez discuss their struggle against stereotypes and how they attempt to maintain ties to their cultures. Lara insists that though she experiences alienation from herself and her cultural community, she struggles against this by returning "to indigenous and mestiza spiritual knowledge for empowerment—knowledge powerful enough to survive despite patriarchal and colonial efforts at destruction" (434). Lara also acknowledges and accepts her mixed-race ancestry, noting that she, too, has the blood of the "white man" (her great-great-grandfather, Luis Arellanes) running through her veins. De la tierra also struggles with the alienation she experiences once in graduate school. Like Lara, de la tierra is faced with a program dominated by British literature and white heterosexual professors and graduate students. Anne-Marie Nuñez and Elizabeth Murakami-Ramalho explain that "at least two decades of research on diversity in higher education indicate that increasing the presence of Latino faculty in higher education is critical to promoting Latino students' educational attainment. Latino faculty understands the cultural backgrounds of Latino students and can serve as role models for them" (4). However, such disappointment on both Latinas' parts encourages each woman to seek other ways of negotiating through academia.

De la tierra negotiates her way through academia by bonding with "select Others in the program," eventually forming "WCC (women of color corner)," thus emphasizing the notions of community and kinship. De la tierra further explains that her group performed their work at a local art gallery, reading "This Frontier Called My Lengua: A Reading by Linguistic Terrorists" to survive (363). De la tierra navigates through an uninviting academic program by bonding with Chicanas in an analogous situation. She utilizes her position as a teacher to empower herself and attain agency as she chooses her multicultural reader, revealing her sexual orientation in the classroom and inviting students to play with languages including Spanish, English, and caló. Incorporating traditional lesson plans with her ideas of what it means to teach, bringing her cultural identity into the classroom embodies adopting a mestizaje of epistemologies.

Similarly, Lara learns how to negotiate her way through academia by first becoming aware of academia's belief in the split between the body, mind, and spirit. Once she acknowledges this fact, Lara contests it by invoking the presence of "all bodies, spirits, and consciousness engaged in similar healing battles," a perfect example of Rendón's sentipensante pedagogy (436). Lara incorporates spirituality into her academic work by refusing to engage in the paradigm of the mind, spirit, and body split and engaging in transformative spiritual work. In short, she refuses to eliminate her identity from academia, including the spiritual aspects of herself, thus adopting a mestizaje of epistemologies.

Similarly, Alvarez describes the alienation she experiences as she attempts to fight the stereotypes imposed on her by her academic community. Alvarez explains that she often had to fight off "their stereotypical conceptions of my cultural and academic identity. As an Ivy League student, I was not a member of the 'underclass' that represented 'the community' to them. Yet I was Puerto Rican enough to be told not to do my dissertation on the Puerto Rican linguistic practices if I wanted to be legitimated as a scholar in my field" (182). As with Lara and de la tierra, Alvarez's entrance into graduate school forces her to confront stereotypes imposed by the instructors, curriculum, and other students. Each woman must contend with making a legitimate claim to their academic abilities while also struggling to retain ties to their community via their research.

Heidi Barajas and Jennifer Pierce's study of Latinas overcoming stereotypes in college reveals that many of the women who relayed their stories of overcoming racism occurred once they found ways to carve out safe spaces where they could "maintain a positive sense of racial ethnic identity" (873). Lara's positive perception of her intellectual abilities and acceptance of her cultural identity allows her to maintain those ties by establishing a safe space. Specifically, Lara engages in Indigenous spirituality, a space where she can balance her cultural and academic self. De la tierra also seeks a safe space to embrace her multiple epistemologies and identities by establishing the women of color corner. Like de la tierra, Alvarez's desire to retain ties to her cultural community encourages her to use it as her research topic and work at the Centro de Estudios Puertorriqueños at CUNY. Rather than choosing one identity or epistemology over the other, Alvarez uses her academic skills to research her community. Similarly, Peña reveals, "I am often asked how I balance activism and academic work. I don't. My rebellion—my social justice work, scholarship, and teaching—are intrinsically linked" (57).

Each woman exhibits an ardent desire to maintain ties to her cultural community, as expressed through the academic work they choose to engage in. This blending of academia and culture allows Lara, Alvarez, and de la tierra to create a third space to weave between their academic and cultural epistemologies.

This space encourages each woman to break free of the stereotypes imposed on them by academia and their cultural identities.

De la tierra adopts a mestizaje of epistemologies once she reflects, "I am the eternal outsider. From within the university system, I carry a prognosis—regardless of how many years I reside here, an integral part of me will always be distant from the mainstream. I will never belong" (358). This statement reveals de la tierra's awareness of the alienation she experiences in academia. It is this awareness that shifts her into the third space of education, where she further acknowledges that "a key part of our evolution lies in our holistic identity, in honoring everything that we are, all of the time"; this includes embracing multiple identities including one's cultural and academic selves and the ways of knowing that accompany each (368). Once again, such awareness emerges as de la tierra engages in the composition and reflection of the oppressions she has encountered.

In this third space, de la tierra can combine her academic skills, as exhibited through critical reflection and composition, with her experiences of oppression. By using the writing and critiquing skills taught to her in academia, de la tierra can contemplate her position as a Chicana lesbian in a predominantly Anglo space. Rather than forsaking her cultural identity and epistemologies, de la tierra balances them with her academic self and ways of knowing. This decision signals an adoption of a mestizaje of epistemologies, which allows de la tierra to become empowered and thus continue her work because she chooses to maintain ties to her community, thereby rejecting the individualistic goals set about by academia.

INTERNALIZING RACISM, CLASSISM, AND SEXISM

While the authors of many of these essays describe how privilege has affected their education and ties to their cultural community, they also discuss the internalization of racism, classism, and sexism. Moraga and Lara both describe the experience of acknowledging and confronting internalized racism. Moraga explains that at the age of twenty-seven, she had to admit that she had "internalized a racism and classism, where the object of oppression is not only someone outside of my skin but the someone inside my skin" (28). Moraga insists that "much of what I value about being Chicana, about my family, has been subverted by Anglo culture and my cooperation with it" (28). Such internalization can be attributed to the schools that Moraga attended, which rich white students dominated. Moraga's conceptualization of internalized racism can also be linked to the pedagogy and structure of the schools themselves.[3] Internalized racism is especially problematic because one begins to adopt the mentality of the oppressor/oppressed paradigm, thereby causing a conflict of identity, such as the education/educación conflict. This conflict ensures that Moraga and other Latinas remain in the oppressor/oppressed paradigm, where they also retain powerlessness, thereby ensuring that the Anglocentric status quo continues unperturbed. Freire notes that oppressed people such as Moraga must choose between being "wholly themselves or being divided," and the division of self eliminates power (48).

Michelle A. Holling's study on racial-ethnic and cultural identifications examines two Chicana college students' perceptions of their identities and the idea of feeling internally divided. Each woman explains that she falls "'prey to the constant battle between the White and Brown,' which the 'outside world' initiates, and that leads to an internal struggle about her identification with both aspects of her identity" (85). Each woman also describes her alienation from her peers and family as she attempts to "straddle both Mexican culture and mainstream American culture" (85). Like the women of Holling's study, Moraga and Lara are forced to battle between their identities and epistemologies because institutions such as schools insist on setting up such binaries as the only method of understanding.

Lara also reveals her experience with the "internalized white man in me" (433). While at Stanford, Lara encounters racism and sexism but notes that she does not speak up. Her inability to speak out against such injustices causes her to reflect: "Why can't I speak in class? Why can't I write as easily as everyone else can? Why can't I feel this place belongs to me, too?" (433). Such questions once again stem from a school system and pedagogies that insist a Latina's cultural knowledge and history are insignificant in academic settings. Vasti Torres notes that Latina students who attend predominantly white institutions feel that they must learn "'to play the game' even when they disagree with the institutional values the faculty represent" (139). Exposure to predominantly white

---

3. L. M. Padilla defines internalized racism as "the acceptance of stereotypes and discriminatory notions that casts one's own racial community as subhuman, inferior, incapable, or a burden on society" (65).

institutions challenges students, especially doctoral students, to "rethink their Bicultural Orientation toward a more Anglo-oriented value system, thereby becoming more consistent with their new academic environment . . . The need for guidance prompts Latina/o doctoral students to believe they need to transform themselves into the school their faculty members want or leave; this need to transform can be even more intense for students in elite research programs" (139). Because the structure of academia often causes Latinas to question their identities, especially if they desire to retain their cultural selves, Latinas such as Moraga and Lara begin to question their abilities. The feelings of insignificance also alienate Moraga and Lara from academia, placing them in the margins, where they soon believe they belong. Internalized racism also leads to a questioning of one's cultural identity and whether there is a place for it in academia.

To deal with internalized racism, Lara employs the use of a mestizaje of epistemologies as a strategy that helps her negotiate such oppression. Lara's employment of a mestizaje of epistemologies begins as she acknowledges that her voice, and therefore her connection to her cultural self and epistemologies, has been silenced by the epistemologies of her school. She describes the sense of alienation she feels as she is denied a chance to voice her opinions: "I have swallowed his racist, sexist, homophobic, classist, and capitalist values and definitions of success. At times, I have also regurgitated them—mostly against myself" (433).

Such feelings and questions propel Lara into the third space of education, where she begins to question whether her identity and her culture's epistemologies have a place in her academic life and vice versa. In this space, Lara reaches the consciousness of her position between multiple identities and epistemologies, which allows her to realize, "Like other people of mixed race before me, I work to make peace with them. Because not to acknowledge and love all who I am is to be defeated, again" (434). Lara also notes such work is "healing work" and "my tools are my words. The tools of neither the oppressed nor the oppressor 'locked in mortal combat,' but simultaneously of and beyond both in the creation of a third transformative space" (434). In the third transformative space, Lara embraces and balances both her cultural and academic identities and epistemologies by first questioning those ideologies that caused her to question her identity and epistemologies in the first place. Like Anzaldúa and Moraga, she utilizes writing to develop a mestizaje of epistemologies, which heals the education/educación conflict.

Lara resists succumbing ultimately to assimilation, her academic self, and the "fragmenting processes of academia" by "consciously nurturing [her] reasoning abilities, spiritual strengths, and the wisdom of [her] body" (437). This is strikingly like Emma Pérez's discussion of the necessity of working to bring "herstories" to light. However, Lara's focus does not rest solely in "herstory"; instead she draws on the spiritual knowledge of her indigenous identity. Lara's development of a mestizaje of epistemologies is necessary to embrace these multiple identities and epistemologies. Specifically, the mestizaje of epistemologies allows her to develop a differential consciousness, allowing Lara, Anzaldúa, and Moraga to weave between various ideologies. Sandoval explains that

> differential consciousness requires grace, flexibility, and strength: enough strength to confidently commit to a well-defined structure of identity for one hour, day, week, month, year; enough flexibility to self-consciously transform that identity according to the requisites of another oppositional ideological tactic if readings of power's formation requite it; enough grace to recognize alliance with others committed to egalitarian social relations and race, gender, sex, class, and social justice, when these other readings of power call for alternative oppositional stands. (*Methodology* 59)

Thus, as Lara, Anzaldúa, and Moraga utilize a mestizaje of epistemologies, which requires a differential consciousness to weave between multiple identities and knowledge, they understand that a balance between the knowledge of their home and of their schools is possible. Accepting this balance ensures that Latinas such as Lara, Anzaldúa, and Moraga feel secure in their identities and epistemologies and, therefore, are empowered.

ACHIEVING AWARENESS AND ADOPTING A MESTIZAJE OF EPISTEMOLOGIES

While I have pointed out the various complexities that accompany the education/educación conflict, including language, privilege, internalized racism, and the struggle against stereotypes, it is also necessary to point out how each Latina begins to overcome the education/educación conflict academia has placed her in. The first step toward overcoming the conflict is achieving awareness, which occurs in the third space of education. Anzaldúa's explanation of the conocimiento path may help me better articulate what the third space of education looks like. Anzaldúa indicates that many of us, especially Latinas, struggle to understand the world we reside in and how our identity is shaped and affected by it. I argue that some Latinas encounter this desire to understand their world and identity primarily through their experiences with the U.S. education system. In attempting to answer the question of who we are and how our identity affects us, it is necessary to understand the first few steps in the path of conocimiento.

Latinas encounter the first stage when they encounter physical, mental, or emotional traumas such as racism, sexism, and other oppressions because of their immersion into an Anglocentric system of education. Because of these traumas, Latinas are then shifted "into the crack between the worlds, shattering the mythology that grounds [them]" (Anzaldúa, "Now Let Us" 544). The shattered mythology is the belief that they must assimilate and reject their cultural epistemologies. Latinas are also forced to confront the fact that engaging with the U.S. education system not only requires assimilation as a marker of success but is also evidence of the rejection of one's Latina identity. This shift also forces a Latina to reach the awareness that her subjectivity is constructed by sexist and racist concepts held by an Anglocentric education system.

Those Latinas who encounter traumatic experiences in K–12 and academia may then shift into this second stage, an in-between space, the third space of education. It is here that Latinas begin to contemplate "the ways [they] construct knowledge, identity, and reality, and explore how some of [their]/others' constructions violate other people's ways of knowing" (Anzaldúa, "Now Let Us" 544). Latinas contemplate the privilege of institutional education over educación. Here, they begin to understand that their identities as Latinas are also deemed inferior by their education system, as revealed through the lack of literature, history, and theory written by and representative of Latinas. In this third space of education, a shift occurs between epistemologies, specifically the school and culture. This shifting and negotiating between cultural and institutional ways of knowing can emerge as a mestizaje of epistemologies, a balance of cultural and school epistemologies and identities.

Each author experiences the education/educación conflict, and once aware of it, she is shifted into the third space of education, where she begins to adopt a mestizaje of epistemologies. Whether at school or home, each woman begins to realize the importance of balancing the epistemologies of each environment and her multiple identities. The women realize there is no need to maintain the binary thought process, which identifies their many identities as unfavorable. Thus, adopting a mestizaje of epistemologies gives each Latina scholar the confidence and ability to accept multiple identities while remaining connected to her family and cultural community. This reestablished or maintained connection allows Latinas to reject the individualistic way of thinking promoted by U.S. school systems instead of collective efforts that will enable them to share their experiences and knowledge with family and their cultural communities. Power emerges from accepting their multiple identities and epistemologies and retaining communal ties.

In addition to noting the shift of each author into the third space of education, where they adopt a mestizaje of epistemologies, the format of their experiences, the testimonio, is further indicative of adopting a mestizaje of epistemologies. Using the testimonio format allows Anzaldúa, Moraga, Alvarez, de la tierra, Lara, and Fiol-Matta to share their educational experiences as Latinas. In choosing to write about these experiences and sharing them with others, each author can demonstrate her growth and transformation through the awareness of the education/educación conflict and the ability to begin overcoming it via a mestizaje of epistemologies. In sharing these experiences, each woman calls on readers to reflect upon their own experiences in K–12 and academia, inviting them to engage in a mestizaje of epistemologies.

The transformation of each Latina author may, in turn, affect those she encounters: students, colleagues, family, organizations to which she belongs, and cultural communities. In this way, Latinas may begin to alter their understanding of what academia is, a place where privileging of individualistic thinking and alienation from culture and family is encouraged; and what it could be, a space where the experiences of Latinas, the working class, and queer people are just as significant as the patriarchal, Anglo, upper-class, heterosexual culture's knowledge. Through reading and analysis of testimonios such as those I have chosen to examine in this chapter, readers begin to realize "there is a need to recognize both the historical absence and invisibility of specific knowledge in essential debates in education and society and the resulting ethnocentric blindness and arrogance in mainstream knowledge systems in the belief that only one knowledge system can 'get it right'" (Andreotti and de Souza 236). Such recognition and acceptance signal the beginnings of adopting a mestizaje of epistemologies in academia, which proposes that privileging be eradicated in favor of a new system of thinking that invites all to share their knowledge. In this way, academia may become more accepting of numerous ways of knowing, especially from those individuals such as Latinas who have struggled to have their voices heard. A mestizaje of epistemologies seeks to stop dividing those in academia and instead encourages working together to bring about social justice for all students in K–12 and academia.

These education testimonios demonstrate how Anzaldúa, Moraga, Alvarez, de la tierra, Lara, and Fiol-Matta can sufficiently navigate between multiple epistemologies and identities. The ability to engage in more than academic work, represented by the acts of writing and reflecting combined with the testimonios of their lived experiences, demonstrates their capacity to balance cultural and academic epistemologies. This balancing of multiple ways of knowing further allows these Latina academics the opportunity to embrace their various identities, thereby providing examples for others to also engage in the healing that accompanies acceptance of one's whole self, as Anzaldúa indicates in her assertion that mestizas must engage in "healing the split" (*Borderlands* 102). This healing on an individual level may empower Latinas to invite the community to mend and become whole, thereby empowering all.

This chapter has allowed me to explore Latina education testimonios and the effects on Latina identity and epistemologies, revealing how Latinas in K–12 and academia can develop a mestizaje of epistemologies to heal the education/educación conflict. In the concluding chapter, I will critically analyze contemporary education testimonios of my self-identifying Latina students. I will use these testimonios/interviews to demonstrate how the education/educación conflict persists and how Latina students employ methods that blend their home/cultural epistemologies with the epistemology of school via a mestizaje of epistemologies. I will compare these recent education testimonios with those presented in this chapter to reveal how the education/educación conflict has shifted but continues to be a major problem in the U.S. education system. I will end with reflections on why a mestizaje of epistemologies is especially critical for those of us teaching and learning in Texas and beyond as we continue to encounter discrimination and systemic racism in K–12 and academia.

5

NI DE AQUÍ, NI DE ALLÁ

Contending with the Education/Educación Conflict and Transforming the Classroom into the Third Space of Education

While chapter 4 examined education testimonios from three pivotal Latina/Chicana feminist literary collections, chapter 5 seeks to continue the analysis of the education/educación conflict and how Latina and Chicana students employ a mestizaje of epistemologies through their education journeys at home and in school. I will also discuss how I employ a mestizaje of epistemologies in my classes to help students navigate the knowledge and learning of their home and school environments. I conducted a qualitative study for this chapter by interviewing students from my Mexican American literature course. Students were provided with eleven questions via email, asking them to address how they balance and retain their cultural/home epistemologies within academia. Through the responses to these questions, students provided education testimonios that aid understanding of how contemporary Latina and Chicana students navigate the education system while retaining ties to their cultural communities. These testimonios will be analyzed and compared to the testimonios provided in the previous chapter, focusing on what I refer to as the education/educación conflict in which Latinas/Chicanas encounter a struggle between their home/cultural knowledge versus the Anglocentric pedagogies and epistemologies espoused in the U.S. school system (K–12 and higher education). I further posit that many Latina/Chicana students today learn specific strategies—such as a mestizaje of epistemologies, a blending of the home/cultural epistemologies with those of school—to negotiate their identities and cultures in these Anglocentric academic spaces, allowing the student to "take home" what they have learned about school and "bring" what they have learned at home to the classroom.

My framework for this study is further guided by *Chicana/Latina Education in Everyday Life: Feminista Perspectives on Pedagogy and Epistemology* (2006), co-edited by Dolores Delgado Bernal et al., in which the editors and authors argue for the necessity of including Chicana and Latina students' lived experiences in education. This collection of essays attempts to focus on "how [Chicanas/Latinas] experience educational institutions as brown people between nations in a racialized society... [and] redefining Chicana/Latinas' everyday experiences, and practices of teaching, learning, and communal 'knowing' as education" (2-3). In addition, the editors assert that the purpose of gathering these educational experiences is to acknowledge that they serve as "theories and methods with vital significance to the field of education and feminist thought" (3). Following these objectives, the interviews I conducted with my students also serve to highlight the educational experiences of Chicana/Latina education experiences eighteen years after the work of Bernal and her associates. Though only four interviews are presented here, the interviewees' experiences and testimonios are significant because they highlight how Chicana/Latina students balance their cultural and educational experiences while seeking survival strategies to help them navigate the system of education that continues to perpetuate assimilationist pedagogies. Thus, the quality of these testimonios rather than the quantity will be the main focus of this study.

This study examines explicitly how Anglocentric, assimilationist pedagogies and epistemologies in the U.S. education system directly impact Latina/Chicana students' identity and cultural ties. I analyze the following questions: How do the current pedagogies and epistemologies of the U.S. education system affect Latina/Chicana students regarding their identities and ties to their culture? What strategies do Latina/Chicana students develop in the face of Anglocentric pedagogies to allow them the means to navigate the school system while retaining ties to their cultural identities and communities? How might students employ multiple epistemologies (a mestizaje of epistemologies) to achieve a balance of knowledge acquired in schools versus at home?

STUDENT BACKGROUNDS

To address the abovementioned questions, I sought volunteers among my Mexican American literature students after gaining Institutional Review Board approval for the study. Five students volunteered to provide their education testimonios via the written interview process, though ultimately, I heard back from only four in time for this study. All students self-identify in some way as Hispanic and Mexican American, though two of the four identify as both Mexican American and Anglo-American. These students range in age from eighteen to twenty-two, and most are classified as sophomores or juniors. Most of the students had also taken multiple classes with me before the Mexican American literature class, and therefore, we have established a specific rapport. Three students are declared English majors, while one is a psychology major who is obtaining a Mexican American studies certificate. Two students hope to attend law school after graduation to focus on immigration law. All students are female and identify as cisgender heterosexual women. None of the four students identify as first generation. Most are second-generation, and at least three of them have parents with master's degrees or higher education degrees. Most students identify as bilingual and can fluently speak Spanish and English. However, most have explained that their dominant language has become English since entering the school system, and most students also indicate that they often use Spanglish at home and with friends. Two students indicated that Spanish is the primary language they utilize in the home environment. For confidentiality, students' names and other identifying factors will not be referenced throughout this analysis. Instead, these students will be referred to by numbers. I will focus on their experiences with the education/educación conflict and a mestizaje of epistemologies in the classroom and at home, though not all admit to having encountered overt examples of this conflict, which I referred to as cultural conflict through the questionnaire. These students' diverse experiences concerning their cultural identity, retaining their culture, and strategizing ways to maintain these things in an Anglocentric school system are significant in and of themselves because they help to understand how educators might improve the education of Latina/Chicana students.

STUDENT #1'S TESTIMONIO AND THE EDUCATION/EDUCACIÓN CONFLICT

Students were asked a series of questions that revolved around the issue of cultural conflict, which I call the education/educación conflict. This issue was defined as a sense of not belonging in a particular space, such as school, because of how one identifies ethnically, culturally, or racially. I directly posed the following questions regarding cultural conflict to each student: "Have you ever encountered cultural conflict at school, a feeling of not quite belonging because of your race or ethnicity?" and "How did you deal with any feelings of cultural conflict? What solutions or strategies did you employ?" While not all students encountered cultural conflict in the school setting, most of them indicated they had experienced some systemic discrimination because of their identities as Mexican Americans or Hispanics. One student, who identified as both Mexican American and Anglo, noted that her feelings of not belonging stemmed from the Anglo community rather than the Mexican American community and culture with which she more closely identifies. This student further elaborated that her sense of not belonging at school emerged primarily through language in instances when she attempted to speak Spanish at school and was reprimanded:

> I am half white and half Mexican but grew up much closer to my Mexican culture. I have never had experiences where people have made me feel like I don't belong in the Latino community. My experiences of cultural conflict have been from feelings of not belonging in an Anglo community. I think the main issues of cultural conflict in school have come through language. I have been told not to speak Spanish several times in school, but a few stood out to me. In high school I was asked by a teacher not to speak Spanish because speaking English was "common decency." It bothered me because saying that it was "common decency" to speak a certain language made no sense especially considering that my school was primarily Latino. It also bothered me that the teacher did not tell students not to speak other languages, but she would tell students not to speak Spanish. In middle school I was told by a teacher that it was "against the rules" to speak Spanish which bothered me because it made it seem like it was against the rules to be Latino in the setting that I was in. Being told not to speak Spanish made me feel that I did not belong because Spanish is tied so closely with my culture. Speaking Spanish not only made me feel connected to my culture but also my Latino friends.[4]

This example shows how this student faced cultural conflict in the classroom via language discrimination. Especially striking is the student's revelation that

---

4. For the sake of accuracy, I have not altered students' responses in any way. I simply copied exactly what they wrote down as they expressed themselves.

the school she attended was primarily Latinx, suggesting that the problem of privileging English over Spanish in the school setting emerges even in spaces where most students and teachers identify as Latinx. This student's testimonio is comparable to similar instances of the language binary system of thought where English is privileged over Spanish, as seen in previous examples from testimonios by Cherríe Moraga and Gloria Anzaldúa. Of note is that these experiences are similar, though decades have passed since Moraga and Anzaldúa experienced the same language discrimination described by this student. The education/educación conflict persists in school systems, as the student notes that the Spanish language was and is crucial to her because it gives her a sense of community and connection to her culture and friends. In this instance, the student's teachers and the system suggested that the education she receives in school, namely via the use of the English language, is the "correct" manner of communication in contrast to Spanish.

STUDENT #2'S TESTIMONIO AND THE EDUCATION/EDUCACIÓN CONFLICT

The second student interviewed regarding the questions of cultural conflict identified as Hispanic and Mexican American. Though she explained that she has chiefly felt welcome in the schools she attended, she did note an instance of cultural conflict similar to the previous student's testimonio. Student #2 noted experiencing microaggressions in the form of mispronouncing her name. Though the student seemingly brushes off the microaggression as a minor problem, one can clearly understand that it was bothersome to her: "I haven't encountered any major cultural conflict at school. The only minor conflict is that some professors and students don't know how to pronounce my name with a rolled r, but other than that I feel pretty welcomed." When the students are asked to contemplate any cultural conflicts they have experienced, they seemingly discount name mispronunciation as one, yet it is troubling enough to mention. Though the student does not refer to this experience as a microaggression, the definition of *microaggression* and the history behind name mispronunciation for ethnic minorities, especially Latinxs, is a long one that has been deeply steeped in the education system and academia. Noted scholars Rita Kohli and Daniel G. Solórzano explain the importance of correctly pronouncing individuals' names, whether in the school environment or beyond, and the dire effects of mispronouncing those names:

> A child begins to understand who they are through their parents' accent, intonation and pronunciation of their name. Additionally, names frequently carry cultural and family significance. Names can connect children to their ancestors, country of origin or ethnic group, and often have deep meaning or symbolism for parents and families. When a child goes to school and their name is mispronounced or changed, it can negate the thought, care and significance of the name, and thus the identity of the child. This happens for white and nonwhite children alike. However, the fact that this experience occurs within a context of historical and continued racism is what makes the negative impact of this experience so powerful for Students of Color. (441)

Thus, in mispronouncing a name, whether intentionally or not, educators suggest to their students that those connections and backgrounds from which their names are derived are insignificant in a school setting. This may also lead to a conflict of identity for the student, especially considering the notion of the education/educación conflict. Kohli and Solórzano further reveal that

> the practice of racialized renaming has been ongoing in the United States history. In the seventeenth through nineteenth centuries, because they were seen as property, enslaved Africans were forced to shed their names, and were given the name of their masters. The names of indigenous people were replaced with Anglo and Christian names until the 1920s ... In 2009, during House testimony on voter identification legislation, a Texas lawyer argued that voters of Asian-descent should adopt names that are "easier for Americans to deal with." (444)

The practice of renaming and mispronouncing names continues today, as evidenced by the student mentioned earlier in her testimonio. Furthermore, such testimonios reveal these mispronunciations to be examples of racial microaggressions defined by Kohli and Solórzano as "*subtle verbal and non-verbal insults/assaults* directed toward People of Color ... *Layered insults/assaults* based on one's race, gender, class, sexuality, language, immigration status, phenotype, accent, or name ... [and] *Cumulative insults/assaults* that take their toll on People of Color" (447). In this instance, we can classify the mispronunciation of the student's name as a racial microaggression even though the student does not identify it as such. However, as the research shows, persistent mispronunciation of one's name eventually takes a toll on a student's sense of cultural identity, perhaps even leading to an education/educación conflict in which she questions whether she belongs in an academic space.

STUDENT #3'S TESTIMONIO AND THE EDUCATION/EDUCACIÓN CONFLICT

Like student #2, student #3 also notes that she has not encountered any overt examples of the education/educación conflict; she attributes this to the fact that she attended school in San Antonio, Texas, where students, faculty, and staff predominantly identify as Latinx. Though this student does not experience cultural conflict in school, she does note that she has experienced this in the workplace through racist comments she overhears. I include student #3's testimonio to juxtapose it against the other testimonios in which students call out the education/educación conflict they have encountered in school, demonstrating that these experiences are not universal to the Latinx community.

STUDENT #4'S TESTIMONIO AND THE EDUCATION/EDUCACIÓN CONFLICT

Student #4 also discusses a form of the education/educación conflict she has encountered at school. Though her example of cultural conflict is not one that takes place directly in the classroom, she does note that she has experienced this conflict when among new friends as she began college:

> One encounter that stood out to me and checked my privilege for me happened my freshman year. I became friends with a girl in my dorm hall. She was Caucasian, but that didn't factor into our friendship at first. I am light-complected and am white-passing, and she mistook that for a different friendship. At first, it was subtle jabs to minority groups, those comments you want to question but don't want to seem rude for insinuating. Then, it was a comfort in making racial jokes. At first, I tried to take it as something we could both learn from and tried to explain that those jokes aren't funny anymore.

The student goes on to note that this experience helped her to recognize the kind of privilege she may have come to the table with as a Mexican American woman who can pass as a white woman because of her light skin. In presenting as white and then being part of conversations where people assumed they could make racist jokes around her, this student notes that her privilege was "checked," or she became aware of it because of the supposed comfort of her "friend" in sharing racist ideas. However, the student resists such privileging and calls out her friend, demonstrating an awareness and a need to push back against such racist jokes despite her ability to pass as white. Like Moraga, this student takes note of her white privilege as someone who can pass as white and uses it to call out racism.

STUDENT NEGOTIATION STRATEGIES AND A MESTIZAJE OF EPISTEMOLOGIES

After these students were asked to take a moment to contemplate how they have encountered the education/educación conflict, they were also asked to consider what strategies and solutions they employed to deal with this issue. Specifically, students were asked, "How did you deal with any feelings of cultural conflict? What solutions or strategies did you employ?" The students' answers varied, ranging from describing confrontation with those discriminating against them and causing cultural conflict to describing journaling or accepting what they seemingly believed they could not change. Student #1 explains what she did to confront those who were discriminating against her and the consequences of such actions:

> Before, I would deal with feelings of cultural conflict by directly confronting the issue. For example, in the high school experience that I explained, I told my teacher that she was being racist. I think the confrontation did work in some cases but not in all. Now in cases of cultural conflict I try to understand that the people who think certain ways are just uneducated/ignorant. I also find that it helps to talk to people like my boyfriend or my mom (both Latino) about how the conflicts make me feel. I think the biggest thing that helps in feelings of cultural conflict is to find solidarity with others from my community.

The student's observation is fundamental, and her methods of pushing against cultural conflict have shifted. These observations signal an essential part of the education/educación conflict as the student shifts consciousness about her positionality in the classroom and society, revealing how she begins to employ a mestizaje of epistemologies through consciousness-raising, taking comfort from her community, and remaining focused on her goals. Though the student indicates that her first responses included confrontation, she notes that sometimes this does not work. Instead, this student becomes more conscious of the complexities surrounding the sense of not belonging and the discrimination she faces.

In considering how student #1 further contemplates the strategies she employs when confronted with the education/educación conflict, I also asked her to contemplate whether people should retain their cultural identities even in conflict and why she believes this may or may not be necessary. In response to this question, the student noted that it was important for people to retain their cultural identities despite obstacles. Of particular importance is her observation regarding the effects that rejection or loss of identity can impart: "I think if one loses their identity in conflict, they lose pieces of themselves that are so important in explaining who they are. By losing one's identity, they could become culturally lost and then internalize the ideas of those that have excluded them. By retaining identity individuals are breaking cycles of assimilation and internalized racism." Such comments reveal the awareness necessary to begin to balance education with educación, as the student notes that cultural identity is essential to retain because rejecting or losing it is part of the larger cycles of systemic racism, including assimilation and internalized racism.

STUDENTS #2 AND #3 NEGOTIATION STRATEGIES AND A MESTIZAJE OF EPISTEMOLOGIES

Similarly, student #2 was asked the same questions about negotiating education/educación and cultural conflicts and their strategies to retain ties to their culture. Student #2 indicates a similar form of awareness as student #1. However, she attempts a more subtle approach: "I usually just remind myself that usually people are not trying to offend me, it's just a matter of being raised differently. Sometimes I try to help people if they want to learn how to pronounce my name in Spanish, but if that has no success, I ask them to pronounce my name without a rolled r or one of my nicknames like T." Student #2 not only shows a level of consciousness-raising in noting that some people may be unaware that they are asserting a racial microaggression but she also attempts to push back against them. At the same time, she notes that sometimes these strategies do not work, and she must compromise to an extent by offering name alternatives. Though this might seem like she is giving in, I suggest that this is more of a compromise, an example of strategic essentialism, a blending of education/educación, allowing this student to retain ties to her cultural identity and find a way to navigate the education system. In considering the importance of cultural identity in the face of conflict, this student also notes, "Yes, I believe people should retain their cultural identities in conflict because as society progresses, we are responsible for cultural and ethnic accountability. Conflict is never going to get resolved if people continue to submit to one race/cultural identity." Like student #1, student #2 notes the importance of cultural identity, once again suggesting that rejecting or losing connections to it might continue to add to larger systemic oppressions. This student further suggests that retaining cultural identities may lead to confronting such cultural conflicts and more significant issues such as systemic racism and discrimination in the school setting. Student #2 further suggests that adhering to the idea of a monolithic cultural or racial identity, as with Anglocentrism, will continue to exacerbate conflict.

Like student #2, student #3 indicates that she has not encountered any cultural conflict in school. However, she attributed this to having lived in San Antonio, Texas (a predominantly Hispanic population), and having attended schools with primarily Hispanic / Mexican American students and teachers her entire life. Though she admits that no major cultural conflicts have interfered with her schooling, she does note that when experiencing troubles with school, she journals in the morning to work through her feelings or turns to reading books as a form of escape. Notably, not all these students directly encountered cultural conflict in their K–12 and higher education experiences, demonstrating that Latinas' schooling experiences are not homogeneous. Many factors play into inevitable cultural conflicts students may or may not encounter. Furthermore, students' willingness to assimilate to different degrees may also impact whether they experience cultural strife or not, just as we see described in the testimonios of the Latina Feminist Group. However, like her counterparts, student #2 believes that people should retain their cultural identities even in the face of conflict, something she has focused on in her research:

> Yes, people should retain their cultural identities even in conflict. Some of the strongest people I know have faced conflict due to their culture. When I asked

them why or how they held on to their cultural identities, they reminded me that their culture was something they could not control and could either embrace it or forget about it. Although I have not faced conflict due to my cultural identity in school, I have in the work environment. It would be easier to forget about my cultural identity to fit in. Still, I believe that if we want to see a change in the environment, we have to accept our cultural identity and embrace it so others will as well.

In noting the importance of culture, each student desires to retain her culture and identity, suggesting that embracing and fighting for one's cultural identity is tied to more significant societal problems that lead to acceptance and inclusion.

A MESTIZAJE OF EPISTEMOLOGIES: BLENDING HOME/CULTURAL KNOWLEDGE WITH EDUCATION

In addition to the students being aware of the importance of their cultural identities, as revealed through each response, they were also asked to contemplate how they bring cultural knowledge to the classroom from their home communities and how they bring the knowledge attained in schools to their homes, namely in what I am referring to as a mestizaje of epistemologies. In each case, students indicated that allowing room to discuss culture and experiences in classroom environments was important, providing a safe space to learn more about their cultures and others. As for how they bring what they learn from school home, each student indicated that dialogue was crucial in discussing many topics, such as intergenerational trauma, at home around the kitchen table or with significant others and friends. Student #1 reveals how she brings her cultural knowledge to the classroom:

> I think the best way to bring cultural knowledge to the classroom is to talk about culture and reflect on experiences. As a student this can be done by explaining and connecting cultural stories to whatever is being talked about in class. On the other hand, for teachers it's important that they make sure to broaden the topics that are discussed and allow students to express their culture. Teachers should be able to inform students on culturally diverse topics within what they are teaching rather than focusing on a whitewashed way of teaching. It's important to allow students to express their cultures while also providing a space where they can learn more about their culture. Examples of this may include

reading culturally relevant books, teaching the truth in history, teaching about important culturally relevant individuals, and so much more.

In short, student #1 suggests that both student and teacher should share the responsibility of embarking on conversations about culture and what she refers to as "culturally diverse topics." Also critical is her nuanced understanding that the stage must be set to help students feel comfortable expressing their cultures and learning more about themselves and others. In contemplating how she brings home what she learns at school, student #1 notes,

> Personally, I bring what I've learned at school home / to my communities by talking about it. I've had so many conversations with my family about topics that I've learned about in class. The biggest thing that I talk about with my family is history. It's interesting because learning about the history of certain events or ideas and taking it home to my family gives my family a lot of "aha moments." The more I discuss the history, the more my family and I are able to understand why they've experienced certain things. With my boyfriend I do talk about a lot of history, but I also tend to share ideas such as generational cycles and just sort of understand why Latinos undergo certain circumstances more than others and why families have certain characteristics. Overall, I think the biggest way that I share what I learn is just through communicating it. In my opinion it's very important to talk and have conversations where my community and I are able to learn together and from one another. On the other hand, I do think that it can be hard to bring knowledge from school to the Latino community. There are problems with Latinos accepting things for "just being that way" and when you try to explain why things are a certain way it becomes a touchy subject. I think there's also a sense of disloyalty connected with Latinos in higher education. Although Latinos do support each other there are certain circumstances where a Latino with a high education becomes considered as sort of a traitor for assimilating to Anglo standards. With that conflict in place, it can be hard for Latinos to bring what they learn in school back to their communities. In those cases, I still think it's important to have conversations about what has been learned but I think it is also up to the Latino who is explaining what they've learned to not put themselves in a position of superiority.

While student #1 notes the importance of sharing what she learns from school with her community, she also admits the complexity of obtaining an education and how one might be perceived by that community as a "traitor" in conveying some of that acquired knowledge. Though she admits this may lead to difficult conversations in our communities, especially with immediate families, student #1 notes the importance of continuing these conversations anyway. She further points out that one can find a way to balance cultural/home knowledge with academia by noting,

> The best way to combine the two [cultural knowledge and academia] is by understanding that there doesn't have to be a divide between them. I think that students should understand that cultural knowledge is the same as formal knowledge but just from a different perspective. I think it's also important to understand where our formal knowledge comes from and who has created the roots of our education systems. Students should be able to analyze formal knowledge in the same way that we are taught to analyze our cultural knowledge while also making connections between cultural and formal knowledge.

She further goes on to state that in her particular case, she has managed to maintain a balance between her cultural knowledge and identity while successfully navigating school through Mexican American studies programs:

> A great way that I've been able to keep a connection between school and my culture has been through Mexican American Studies programs. I was initially introduced to Mexican American Studies as a "filler course" in my senior year of high school. I enjoyed the class so much as it gave the opportunity to learn about my culture in a way that I never had before. Once I got to college and found out that St Mary's offered a Mexican American Studies minor, I immediately signed up for it. The Mexican American Studies Minor has enabled me to connect with and learn so much more about my culture. I think that Mexican American Studies programs, and others like it, are so important in supporting cultural learning and connecting it with formal education.

Her last point is particularly poignant given the research on Mexican American studies and ethnic studies, which reveals that such courses often boost high school students' retention and graduation rates.[5] In short, we see the

---

5. Noted scholar Nolan Cabrera has done extensive research on the effects of ethnic studies programs, specifically Mexican American studies classes in Arizona, demonstrating the impact that such classes have on students' education and success. Further information about his data is revealed in "Lies, Damn Lies, and Statistics: The Impact of Mexican American Studies Classes,"

impact that bringing one's culture to school can have on identity, student success, and sense of belongingness, as well as how students consider their future.

These are only a few instances of students who have sometimes encountered cultural conflict in their schooling experiences. Not all students have these experiences, and numerous factors are essential to consider, including regions, family upbringing, and perceptions of the importance of culture, language, and school. These testimonios demonstrate that cultural conflict (the education/educación conflict) persists in our society despite our progress in establishing programs such as Mexican American studies electives in Texas and ethnic studies programs nationwide. At the same time, these testimonios demonstrate the diversity of experiences our students have in the classroom, revealing that there is no one surefire solution to these issues of the education/educación conflict. The strategies students have employed when encountering this conflict blend the epistemologies of the home/culture and school, suggesting that there is a path forward that allows Latinx students to retain ties to their cultures and home communities while navigating the U.S. education system successfully. Though not all students employ or learn strategies such as a mestizaje of epistemologies, I argue that we can teach students to strategically navigate spaces, such as schools, that have a long history of denying and then discriminating against Latinx students, even in education settings that are predominantly occupied by Latinx students, faculty, and staff. This can be done primarily through the use of interdisciplinary approaches that combine disciplines and theories such as literature, history, Chicana third space feminism, and CRT. Furthermore, I argue that the key to developing a mestizaje of epistemologies as a method of resistance and strategy in education lies in establishing a community and safe space in the third space of education where students are invited to celebrate, critique, and share their cultures and cultural selves without judgment or fear.

CENTERING THE CLASSROOM AS A THIRD SPACE OF EDUCATION AND ADOPTING A MESTIZAJE OF EPISTEMOLOGIES AS PEDAGOGY

In attempting to find a term that could accurately describe this experience of the education/educación conflict and overcoming it by utilizing a mestizaje of

---

chapter 2 of *Raza Studies: The Public Option for Educational Revolution*, edited by Julio Cammarota and Augustine Romero.

epistemologies, I developed a list of common themes, emotions, and thoughts expressed by Latina protagonists, writers, and students. Some of the words, phrases, and ideas that the protagonists of *Telling to Live* consistently repeated, as well as terms used in *This Bridge Called My Back*, *This Bridge We Call Home*, and *Golondrina, Why Did You Leave Me?*, include the following: *return, weave, forget, belong, remember, negotiation, struggle, home, past, future, hope, guilt, shame, alienation, family,* and *assimilation,* to name a few. All these terms are at one time mentioned by Latina protagonists, writers, and students to describe the education/educación conflict and a mestizaje of epistemologies. Each describes the pain of forgetting one's native language, culture, and sometimes identity; the struggle to belong to contradictory home and school cultures; the negotiation that occurs between the epistemologies of homes and schools; and the guilt and shame that is often felt when that sense of belonging diminishes and instead becomes alienation from family and self.

Though these writers and protagonists use negative connotations, significantly when associated with their education experiences, many of the words used to describe their dilemma indicate a desire to resist this education/educación conflict. The fact that these protagonists are even contemplating how problematic the education/educación conflict truly is further demonstrates that the authors of such texts are not only aware of such an issue; they, at some point in their lives, have learned how to negotiate their way through it via a mestizaje of epistemologies. In short, the writers and protagonists of such texts have learned that achieving an education is like the weaving of a blanket. To truly achieve an education that does not involve alienation, shame, or guilt, it is necessary to weave together multiple epistemologies.

As the teacher, I am not weaving together these several types of knowledge in this scenario. Instead, I serve as a mentor who guides students in their weaving process. As Rendón describes, I consider my positionality in the classroom as a "teacher/learner, who possesses knowledge and expertise but who also realizes that no one human being knows everything" (138). In playing multiple roles, I am the one who provides new strategies and designs and other knowledge so that students may weave together these various forms of home and school knowledge, experiences, and ways of knowing to interpret better the literature we read. In this way, weaving the student's multiple knowledge may also allow for a better understanding of their world. Thus, the weaving strategies students learn in my classroom can be taken outside to their communities and beyond, allowing them also to become guides for their families, friends, co-workers, and others. Like the protagonists and writers of these researched texts, my students throughout the years have expressed similar feelings of wanting to leave home because of problematic family and cultural dynamics; the works of Gloria E. Anzaldúa speak to students who love their families and communities but do not feel like they completely belong. At the same time, these students also desire to remain with their communities or return to them to help by becoming immigration lawyers, working for non-profits, and becoming teachers. Most recently, in my Women Authors course, my students were introduced to *This Bridge Called My Back*, where we took the time to contemplate the notion of community and how it may support and empower women of color, especially during this trying time in Texas. Overwhelmingly, my students expressed a deep-seated desire to retain ties to their cultures and identities while establishing support systems for women who have endured marginalization at the hands of friends, professors, teachers, and society. Despite these persecutions, students noted that they retained a sense of hope derived from communities such as our classroom and from mentorship they found with me or others.

Serving as a mentor to my students includes incorporating Rendón's sentipensante pedagogy and understanding that it is my responsibility to acknowledge my students' identities. This is an ongoing project that is difficult to maintain; I have encountered students who are dealing with emotional problems, family issues, money troubles, abuse, and countless other issues. The past few years have significantly impacted my students because of civil unrest, political controversies, and a global pandemic. Thus, I have learned that this mestizaje of epistemologies must continually adjust and I must be flexible to the needs of my students. I begin each semester by explaining to my students that I am here to help guide them through this class. They must adhere to specific rules and assignments, but my door is always open. I am willing to listen to what they say so that we might work together to resolve their issues, which are often part of more significant systemic problems that we work to identify and resist through the study of literature, history, and Chicana third space feminism.

A focus on students as whole individuals also allows me to contemplate the multiple types of knowledge and information they come to the classroom with. To teach my students how to weave their multiple knowledges, I expose my students to Latina literature, Chicana third space feminism, and CRT. Especially significant are the theoretical concepts of Gloria Anzaldúa, Emma Pérez, Chela Sandoval, Dolores Delgado Bernal, Daniel Solórzano, and Laura

Rendón. Exposure to such theories models how theories can emerge from our daily lives and demonstrates the need for social justice in the classroom. It is essential to include such theories in my classroom and make them accessible to my students so that they may utilize them to analyze literature and the world. I make these theories accessible to my students by explaining that everyone can engage in theory-making, which occurs when their opinion is asserted via oral or written communication. Many students find the idea that their opinion is just as valuable as prestigious theorists daunting but exciting. However, the use of Chicana third space feminism, especially the theories of Gloria E. Anzaldúa, Cherríe Moraga, and Sonia Saldívar-Hull, points to the importance of questioning what theory is and who creates it. Exploring one's reactions to the literature we read in class yields examples of students engaging in theory without knowing it. In this way, I hope to validate students' cultural epistemologies while teaching them how to achieve consciousness of this fact and engage in further critical analysis via the tools of literary and educational theories. A few activities that I use to stress the equal importance of cultural and institutional epistemologies include small group discussions focusing on the personal connections one makes with the text, discussion board posts, and essays in which students are encouraged to assert and claim their opinions.

I also do not restrict students' discourse in their essays to strictly third-person analyses, often used in English literature and language courses. I invite my students to bring their subjective experiences into their written and oral discussions while encouraging them to seek sources beyond the "traditional" academic databases. Students are often shocked when I say yes, I want to hear and read their opinions because they are just as legitimate and valid as the scholars we read for class. Small group discussions also enable students to create relationships, discover similarities and differences, and learn from each other. My classes are often interdisciplinary, primarily exploring literature but supplemented with history, art, education, and literary theories.

I focus on Chicana and Latina literature by authors such as Barbara Renaud González, Loida Maritza Pérez, Gloria Anzaldúa, Cherríe Moraga, Lorna Dee Cervantes, Sandra Cisneros, and others. Exposing students to such texts, especially with multiple genres represented within single works, also allows me to teach theory in a more accessible way. As Anzaldúa indicates, "you can theorize through fiction and poetry; it's just harder. It's an unconscious kind of process. Instead of coming in through the head with the intellectual concept, you come in through the backdoor with the feeling, the emotion, the experience. But if you start reflecting on that experience, you can come back to the theory" (*Interviews* 263). This is why I begin my classes by pointing out that I focus on literature written by Latinas and Native American women because their voices continue to be silenced not only in the literary world but beyond. Alicia Gaspar de Alba underscores the importance of Chicana literature and their role as writers; I would expand this to include all Latinas, for

> the Chicana writer, like the curandera (medicine woman) or the bruja (witch), is the keeper of the culture, keeper of the memories, rituals, the stories, the superstitions, the language, the imagery of her Mexican heritage. She is also the one who changes the culture, the one who breeds a new language and a new lifestyle, new values, new images, and rhythms, new dreams and conflicts into that heritage making all of this brouhaha and cultural schizophrenia a new legacy for those who have still to squeeze into legitimacy as human beings and American citizens. (245)

It is, therefore, vital to examine Latina literature because, as Gaspar de Alba notes, Latinas are keepers of culture, stories, and advice. They are the ones who can adapt and alter culture yet maintain ties to the traditions so that future generations may "progress" in school and hold on to their cultural identities.

I also stress that though the "traditional" literary canon has undergone many changes, English departments continue to value literature written by Anglo men more than that written by women. I emphasize the works of the women because they provide unique accounts of what it means to be a Latina struggling with attaining a formal education while retaining her cultural identity and epistemology. Using such authors' literary works, I also hope to invite my students to see themselves, their families, their friends, and others in the portrayed characters. In short, I encourage students to reach out, to make those connections, and to resist the problematic binary system of U.S. institutions of learning and society. In this way, I hope to engage in Rendón's sensing/thinking pedagogy, including "eliciting social awareness within the student and teacher and some form of social change in and out of the classroom" (136). Such connections may also encourage my students to understand better what it means to be a Latina in higher education and academia. This invitation may also encourage Latina students who encounter the education/educación conflict to examine their own lives and recognize the need to balance the epistemologies of their schools and homes.

I invite my students not only to use the literary theories we have learned in class but also to make connections to their everyday lives—insisting that they weave together the valuable epistemologies of their home cultures with those of school. One of the best ways to do this is to encourage students to share their experiences, their family stories, and the learning processes of the home. In addition to encouraging such sharing, I also emphasize that the individual experiences my students share are valid methods of critically theorizing literature and our world. Students have shared personal and family stories via discussions and through their writing, which allows connections to be made with other students; this occurs mainly in small group discussions. I have even encouraged code-switching in essays, allowing students to shift between multiple languages and epistemologies to demonstrate their understanding of texts.

This action of weaving a mestizaje of epistemologies encourages my students to return repeatedly to the epistemologies of their home cultures so that they may not forget or feel alienated from their families and cultures. In this way, I transform my classroom into a third space of education, an in-between space where the knowledge of academia and students' cultural communities are equally valid methods of analyzing literature and the world. I utilize literature such as *Borderlands*, *Geographies of Home*, *The House on Mango Street*, and *Golondrina, Why Did You Leave Me?* to validate students' learning. Exposure to such texts invites Latinas to relate to the protagonists and writers and invites all students to learn about other cultures, worlds, and individuals, no matter their cultural background. Such understanding may then include an epiphany regarding the oppressions that continue to exist for Latinas in education and society. This awareness propels students to resist and transform academia for themselves and future generations. Such transformations may eventually expand beyond literature and the classroom, inviting all to "heal the split" imposed on us (Anzaldúa, *Borderlands* 102).

BIBLIOGRAPHY

Acuña, Rodolfo. *Occupied America: A History of Chicanos*. 4th ed., Addison Wesley Longman, 2000.

Alabama State Legislature. House Bill 56, 2011. LegiScan, accessed 5 Sep. 2023, legiscan.com/AL/bill/HB56/2011.

Alarcón, Norma. "Chicana Feminism: In the Tracks of the 'Native Woman.'" *Cultural Studies*, vol. 4, no. 3, 1990, pp. 248–56.

Alberto, Lourdes. "Nations, Nationalism, and Indígenas: The 'Indian' in the Chicano Revolutionary Imaginary." *Critical Ethnic Studies*, vol. 2, no. 1, spring 2016, pp. 107–27.

Alemán, Enrique Jr. *Mexican American School Leadership in South Texas: Toward a Critical Race Analysis of School Finance Policy*. 2004. U of Texas, dissertation. Dissertations and Theses: Full Text, ProQuest.

Alvarez, Celia. "Snapshots from My Daze in School." *Telling to Live: Latina Feminist Testimonios*, edited by the Latina Feminist Group, Duke UP, 2001, pp. 177–84.

Anaya, Rudolfo. *Bless Me, Ultima*. Warner Books Edition, 1994.

Anderson, Perry. "The Antinomies of Antonio Gramsci." *New Left Review*, vol. 100, 1976, pp. 5–78.

Andreotti, Vanessa de Oliveira, and Lynn Mario T. M. de Souza. "Towards Global Citizenship Education 'Otherwise.'" *Postcolonial Perspectives on Global Citizenship Education*, edited by Andreotti and de Souza, Routledge, 2011, pp. 221–38.

Andreotti, Vanessa, et al. "Epistemological Pluralism: Ethical and Pedagogical Challenges in Higher Education." *AlterNative: An International Journal of Indigenous Peoples*, vol. 7, no. 1, 2011, pp. 40–50.

Anzaldúa, Gloria. *Borderlands / La Frontera*. Aunt Lute Books, 1999.

Anzaldúa, Gloria. *The Gloria Anzaldúa Reader*. Edited by AnaLouise Keating, Duke UP, 2009.

Anzaldúa, Gloria. *Interviews/Entrevistas*. Edited by AnaLouise Keating, Routledge, 2000.

Anzaldúa, Gloria. Introduction. *Making Face, Making Soul: Haciendo Caras*, edited by Anzaldúa, Aunt Lute Foundation Books, 1990, pp. xv–xxviii.

Anzaldúa, Gloria. "Now Let Us Shift . . . the Path of Conocimiento . . . Inner Work, Public Acts." *This Bridge We Call Home: Radical Visions for Transformation*, edited by Anzaldúa and AnaLouise Keating, Routledge, 2002, pp. 540–76.

Anzaldúa, Gloria. "Speaking in Tongues: A Letter to Third World Women Writers." *This Bridge Called My Back: Writings by Radical Women of Color*, edited by Cherríe Moraga and Anzaldúa, 3rd ed., Kitchen Table Press, 2002, pp. 183–93.

Anzaldúa, Gloria. "(Un)natural Bridges, (Un)safe Spaces." Preface. *This Bridge We Call Home: Radical Visions for Transformation*, edited by Anzaldúa and AnaLouise Keating. Routledge, 2002, pp. 1–20.

Anzaldúa, Gloria, and Cherríe Moraga. "Entering the Lives of Others: Theory in the Flesh." *This Bridge Called My Back: Writings by Radical Women of Color*, edited by Moraga and Anzaldúa, 3rd ed., Kitchen Table Press, 2002, p. 21.

Arce, Julissa. *You Sound Like a White Girl: A Case for Rejecting Assimilation*. Flatiron Books, 2020.

Barajas, Heidi Lasley, and Jennifer L. Pierce. "The Significance of Race and Gender in School Success Among Latinas and Latinos in College." *Gender and Society*, vol. 15, 2001, pp. 859–78.

Barrera, Cordelia. *The Haunted Southwest: Towards an Ethics of Place in Borderland Literature*. Texas Tech UP, 2022.

Bartlett, Lesley, and Ofelia García. *Additive Schooling in Subtractive Times: Bilingual Education and Dominican Immigrant Youth in the Heights*. Vanderbilt UP, 2011.

Benjamin-Labarthe, Elyette. "Walkout (2006): Moctesuma Esparza's Retrospective Outlook on the Chicano Movement." *Camino Real*, vol. 1, no. 1, 2009, pp. 11–25.

Bernal, Dolores Delgado. "Critical Race Theory, Latino Critical Theory, and Critical Raced-Gendered Epistemologies: Recognizing Students of Color as Holders and Creators of Knowledge." *Qualitative Inquiry*, no. 8, 2002, pp. 105–26.

Bernal, Dolores Delgado. "Grassroots Leadership Reconceptualized: Chicana Oral Histories and the 1968 East Los Angeles School Blowouts." *Frontiers: A Journal of Women Studies*, vol. 19, no. 2, 1998, pp. 113–42. JSTOR, doi.org/10.2307/3347162.

Bernal, Dolores Delgado, et al., editors. "Chicanas/Latinas Building Bridges." *Chicana/Latina Education in Everyday Life: Feminista Perspectives on Pedagogy and Epistemology*, State U of New York P, 2006, pp. 2–3.

Beverley, John. "The Margin at the Center: On *Testimonio* (Testimonial Narrative)." *De/colonizing the Subject: The Politics of Gender in Women's Autobiography*, edited by Sidonie Smith, U of Minnesota P, 1992, pp. 91–144.

Blackwell, Maylei. *¡Chicana Power! Contested Histories of Feminism in the Chicana Movement*. U of Texas P, 2011.

Blake, Debra J. *Chicana Sexuality and Gender: Cultural Refiguring in Literature, Oral History, and Art*. Duke UP, 2008.

Bost, Suzanne. "Transgressing Borders: Puerto Rican and Latina Mestizaje." *MELUS*, vol. 25, no. 2, July 2000, pp. 187–211. EBSCOhost, doi-org.blume.stmarytx.edu/10.2307/468226.
"California Proposition 209, Affirmative Action Initiative (1996)." Ballotpedia, 5 Sep. 2023, ballotpedia.org/California_Proposition_209,_Affirmative_Action_Initiative_(1996).
Candelaria, Cordelia. "La Malinche, Feminist Prototype." *Frontiers: A Journal of Women Studies*, vol. 5, no. 2, 1980, pp. 1–6.
Cantú, Norma E. "Sitio y Lengua: Chicana Third Space Feminist Theory." Keynote talk at the 7th Congreso de Literatura Chicana, 22 May 2010, León, Spain.
Cantú, Norma E. "The Bridge: Chicana Feminist Literary Theory and the Practice of Creating Critical Spaces." *Aztlán: A Journal of Chicano Studies*, vol. 23, no. 2, 1998, pp. 23–47.
Cantú-Sánchez, Margaret. "'The Fourth Choice': Forging the Future of Chicanx Mother/Daughter Relationships Through Storytelling and the Path of Conocimiento in Erika Sánchez's *I'm Not Your Perfect Mexican Daughter* and Barbara Renaud González's *Golondrina, Why Did You Leave Me?*" *Label Me Latina/o: Journal of Twentieth and Twenty-First Centuries Latino Literary Production*, vol. 8, 2018, pp. 1–17.
Cantú-Sánchez, Margaret. "A Mestizaje of Epistemologies in *American Indian Stories* and *Ceremony*." *Nakum*, vol. 2, no. 1, 2011, pp.1–35.
Castellanos, Jeanett, and Alberta M. Gloria. "Latina/o and African American Students at Predominantly White Institutions: A Psychosociocultural Perspective of Cultural Congruity, Campus Climate, and Academic Persistence." *The Majority in the Minority: Expanding the Representation of Latina/o Faculty, Administrators and Students in Higher Education*, edited by Castellanos and Lee Jones, Stylus Publishing, 2003, pp. 71–111.
Castillo, Ana. *Massacre of the Dreamers: Essays on Xicanisma*. Penguin, 1995.
Chavez-Dueñas, Nayeli Y., Hector Y. Adames, and Kurt C. Organista. "Skin-Color Prejudice and Within-Group Racial Discrimination: Historical and Current Impact on Latino/a Populations." *Hispanic Journal of Behavioral Sciences*, vol. 36, no. 1, 2004, pp. 3–26.
Christian, Barbara. "The Race for Theory." *Cultural Critique: The Nature and Context of Minority Discourse*, vol. 6, 1987, pp. 51–63.
Churchill, Ward. "Genocide by Any Other Name." *Kill the Indian Save the Man: The Genocidal Impact of American Indian Residential Schools*, by Churchill, City Light Books, 2004, pp. 1–82.
Cisneros, Sandra. *The House on Mango Street*. Vintage Books, 1984.
Cruz, Cynthia. *Testimonial Narratives of Queer Street Youth: Toward an Epistemology of a Brown Body*. 2006. U of California, Los Angeles, dissertation. Dissertations and Theses: Full Text, ProQuest.
de la tierra, tatiana. "Aliens and Others in Search of the Tribe in Academe." *This Bridge We Call Home: Radical Visions for Transformation*, edited by Gloria E. Anzaldúa and AnaLouise Keating, Routledge, 2002, pp. 358–68.
Delgadillo, Theresa. *Spiritual Mestizaje: Religion, Gender, Race, and Nation in Contemporary Chicana Narrative*. Duke UP, 2011.
Di Iorio, Lyn F. "'That Animals Might Speak': Doubles and the Uncanny in Loida Maritza Pérez' *Geographies of Home*." *Killing Spanish: Doubles, Dead Mothers and Other Allegories of Ambiva-*

lent United States Latina/o Caribbean Identity. 2000. U of California, Berkeley, dissertation. Dissertations and Theses: Full Text, ProQuest.

Di Leo, Jeffrey R. "Hide It from the Kids." *American Book Review*, vol. 33, no. 1, 2011, p. 2. Academic Search Complete, dx.doi.org/10.1353/abr.2011.0152.

DuBois, W. E. B. "Double-Consciousness and the Veil." 1989. *Social Class and Stratification: Classic Statements and Theoretical Debates*, edited by Rhonda F. Levin, Rowman and Littlefield Publishers, 2006, pp. 203–10.

Fanon, Frantz. *Black Skin, White Masks*. Grove, 2008.

Fernandez, Luisa Ochoa. "Family as the Patriarchal Confinement of Women in Sandra Cisneros' *The House of Mango Street* and Loida M. Pérez's *Geographies of Home*." *Evolving Origins, Transplanting Cultures: Literary Legacies of the New Americans*, edited by Antonia Domínguez Miguela and Laura Paloma Alonso Gallo, Servicio de Publicaciones de la Universidad de Huelva, 2001, pp. 119–28.

Fiol-Matta, Liza. "Another Way to Grow Up Puerto Rican." *Telling to Live: Latina Feminist Testimonios*, edited by the Latina Feminist Group, Duke UP, 2001, pp. 192–95.

Flores-González, Nilda. *School Kids/Street Kids: Identity Development in Latino Students*. Teachers College Press, 2002.

Foucault, Michel. *Discipline and Punish: The Birth of the Prison*. Random House, 1995.

Freire, Paulo. *Pedagogy of the Oppressed*. Continuum International Publishing Group, 2000.

Fry, Richard. "Hispanic College Enrollment Spikes, Narrowing Gaps with Other Groups." Pew Hispanic Center on the Web, 25 Aug. 2011, www.pewresearch.org/race-and-ethnicity/2011/08/25/hispanic-college-enrollment-spikes-narrowing-gaps-with-other-groups/.

Garcia, Alma M. *Chicana Feminist Thought: The Basic Historical Writings*. Routledge, 1997.

Garcia, Gina Ann. *Becoming Hispanic-Serving Institutions: Opportunities for Colleges and Universities*. Johns Hopkins UP, 2019.

García, Mario T. *Rewriting the Chicano Movement: New Histories of Mexican American Activism in the Civil Rights Era*. U of Arizona P, 2021. EBSCOhost, research.ebsco.com/linkprocessor/plink?id=ae622ba9-0590-3db0-92b0-78fd3507320f.

Gaspar de Alba, Alicia. "Literary Wetback." *Massachusetts Review*, vol. 29, no. 2, summer 1988, pp. 242–46.

González, Barbara Renaud. *Golondrina, Why Did You Leave Me?* U of Texas P, 2009.

González, Jovita, and Eve Raleigh. *Caballero: A Historical Novel*. Texas A&M UP, 2008.

Gramsci, Antonio. "Hegemony, Intellectuals, and the State." Translated by Quintin Hoare and Geoffrey Nowell-Smith, 1971. *Cultural Theory and Popular Culture: A Reader*, edited by John Storey, 2nd ed., Pearson, 1998, pp. 210–17.

Grande, Sandy. *Red Pedagogy: Native American Social and Political Thought*. Rowman and Littlefield, 2004.

Halperin, Laura. *Narratives of Transgression: Deviance and Defiance in Late Twentieth Century Latina Literature*. 2006. U of Michigan, dissertation. Dissertations and Theses: Full Text, ProQuest.

Hernández-Avila, Inés. "Relocations upon Relocations: Home, Language, and Native American Women's Writing." *Reading Native American Women: Critical/Creative Representations*, Altamira Press, 2005, pp. 171–88.

Herrera, Cristina. "I Stand Here *Limpiando*: Maternal Knowledge, Chicana Subjectivity, and Mother-Daughter Bonding in Bárbara Renaud González's *Golondrina, Why Did You Leave Me?" Women's Studies*, vol. 46, no. 5, July 2017, pp. 442–55. EBSCOhost, https://doi-org.blume.stmarytx.edu/10.1080/00497878.2017.1324444.

Holling, Michelle A. "The Critical Consciousness of Chicana and Latina Students: Negotiating Identity amid Socio-Cultural Beliefs and Ideology." *Chicana/Latina Education in Everyday Life*, edited by Dolores Delgado Bernal et al., State U of New York P, 2006, pp. 81–94.

Hurtado, Aída. *Voicing Chicana Feminisms: Young Women Speak Out on Sexuality and Identity*. New York UP, 2003.

Hurtado, Aída, and Mrinal Sinha. "Differences and Similarities: Latina and Latino Doctoral Students Navigating the Gender Divide." *The Latina/o Pathway to the Ph.D.: Abriendo Caminos*, edited by Jeanette Castellanos, Alberta M. Gloria, and Mark Kamimura. Taylor and Francis Group, 2006, pp. 149–68.

Kauffman, Albert H. "Latino Education in Texas: A History of Systematic Recycling Discrimination." *St. Mary's Law Journal*, vol. 50, no. 3, Jan. 2019, pp. 861–916. EBSCOhost, research.ebsco.com/linkprocessor/plink?id=f3762829-85d2-3c22-a319-70983054b834.

Kohli, Rita, and Daniel G. Solórzano. "Teachers, Please Learn Our Names!: Racial Microaggressions and the K–12 Classroom." *Race, Ethnicity, and Education*, vol. 15, no. 4, pp. 441–62, doi.org/10.1080/13613324.2012.674026.

Krogstad, Jens Manuel. "5 Facts About Latinos and Education." Pew Research Center, 26 July 2016, www.pewresearch.org/short-reads/2016/07/28/5-facts-about-latinos-and-education/.

Lara, Irene. "Healing Sueños for Academia." *This Bridge We Call Home: Radical Visions for Transformation*, edited by Gloria E. Anzaldúa and AnaLouise Keating, Routledge, 2002, pp. 433–38.

Latina Feminist Group. *Telling to Live: Latina Feminist* Testimonios. Duke UP, 2001.

"Latinas at Hispanic-Serving Institutions (HSIs)." Excelencia in Education, accessed 8 Aug. 2024, www.edexcelencia.org/research/fact-sheets/latinas-hispanic-serving-institutions-hsis.

"Latino College Completion: United States." Excelencia in Education, accessed 7 Dec. 2023, www.edexcelencia.org/research/latino-college-completion.

Lavie, Smadar. "Blowups in the Borderzones: Third World Israeli Authors' Gropings for Home." *Displacement, Diaspora, and Geographies of Identity*, edited by Lavie and Ted Swedenburg, Duke UP, 2013, pp. 55–96. EBSCOhost, doi-org.blume.stmarytx.edu/10.2307/j.ctv1168c4d.

Lomawaima, K. Tsianina, and Teresa L. McCarty. "When Tribal Sovereignty Challenges Democracy: American Indian Education and the Democratic Ideal." *American Educational Research Journal*, vol. 39, no. 2, summer 2002, pp. 279–305.

López, Sonia A. "The Role of the Chicana Within the Student Movement." *Chicana Feminist Thought: The Basic Historical Writings*, edited by Alma García, Routledge, 1997, pp. 100–107.

Lorde, Audre. "Age, Race, Class, and Sex: Women Redefining Difference." *Dangerous Liaisons: Gender, Nation, and Postcolonial Perspectives*, edited by Anne McClintock, Aamir Mufti, and Ella Shohat, U of Minnesota P, 1997, pp. 374–80.

Lugones, María. "Playfulness, 'World'-Travelling, and Loving Perception." *Hypatia*, vol. 2, no. 2, summer 1987, pp. 3–19.

MacDonald, Victoria-María. *Latino Education in the United States: A Narrated History from 1513–2000*. Palgrave Macmillan, 2004.

MacDonald, Victoria-María, and Juan F. Carrillo. "The United States of Latinos." *Handbook of Latinos and Education: Theory, Research, and Practice*, edited by Enrique G. Murillo, Routledge, 2010, pp. 8–26.

MacDonald, Victoria-María, and Teresa García. "Historical Perspectives on Latino Access to Higher Education, 1848–1990." *The Majority in the Minority: Expanding the Representation of Latina/o Faculty, Administrators, and Students in Higher Education*, edited by Jeanett Castellanos and Lee Jones, Stylus Publishing, 2003, pp. 15–46.

Martinez, Monica Muñoz. *The Injustice Never Leaves You: Anti-Mexican Violence in Texas*. Harvard UP, 2018.

McMahon, Marci. "Politicizing Spanish-Mexican Domesticity, Redefining Fronteras: Jovita González's *Caballero* and Cleofas Jaramillo's *Romance of a Little Village Girl*." *Frontiers*, vol. 28, nos. 1–2, 2007, pp. 232–54.

Mendez, Susan Carol. "Spirituality and Violence in Loida Maritza Perez's *Geographies of Home*." *Geographies of Spirit: Locating an Afro-Latina/o Diasporic Space in United States Latina/o Literary Studies*. 2005. U of California, Riverside, dissertation.

Mignolo, Walter. "The Enduring Enchantment: (Or the Epistemic Privilege of Modernity and Where to Go from Here)." *The South Atlantic Quarterly*, vol. 101, no. 4, 2002, pp. 937–54.

Miller, Marilyn Grace. *Rise and Fall of the Cosmic Race*. U of Texas P, 2004.

Montejano, David. *Anglos and Mexicans: In the Making of Texas 1836–1986*. UP of Austin, 1987.

Monzó, Lilia D., and Robert S. Rueda. "Professional Roles, Caring, and Scaffolds: Latino Teachers' and Paraeducators' Interactions with Latino Students." *American Journal of Education*, vol. 109, no. 4, Aug. 2001, pp. 438–71.

Mora, Lauren. "Hispanic Enrollment Reaches New High at Four-Year Colleges in the U.S., but Affordability Remains an Obstacle." Pew Research Center, 7 Oct. 2022, www.pewresearch.org/short-reads/2022/10/07/hispanic-enrollment-reaches-new-high-at-four-year-colleges-in-the-u-s-but-affordability-remains-an-obstacle/.

Moraga, Cherríe L. "La Güera." *This Bridge Called My Back: Writings by Radical Women of Color*, edited by Moraga and Gloria Anzaldúa, 2nd ed., Kitchen Table Press, 1983, pp. 24–32.

Moraga, Cherríe, and Gloria Anzaldúa. Introduction, 1981. *This Bridge Called My Back: Writings by Radical Women of Color*, edited by Moraga and Anzaldúa, 3rd ed., Kitchen Table Press, 2002, p. lvi.

Moraga, Cherríe L., and Celia Herrera Rodriguez. *A Xicana Codex of Changing Consciousness: Writings, 2000–2010*. Duke UP, 2011.

Morton, Stephen. *Gayatri Chakravorty Spivak*. Routledge, 2003.

Muñoz, Carlos. *Youth, Identity, Power: The Chicano Movement*. Verso, 1989.

Nieto, Sonia. *Language, Culture, and Teaching*. Lawrence Erlbaum Associates Publishers, 2002.

Nora, Amaury, Libby Barlow, and Gloria Crisp. "An Assessment of Hispanic Students in Four-Year Institutions of Higher Education." *The Latina/o Pathway to the Ph.D.: Abriendo Caminos*, edited by Jeanett Castellanos, Alberta M. Gloria, and Mark Kamimura. Taylor and Francis Group, 2006, pp. 55–77.

Nuñez, Anne-Marie, and Elizabeth Murakami-Ramalho. "The Demographic Dividend: Why the Success of Latino Faculty and Students Is Critical." *Academe Online*, vol. 98, no. 1, Jan.–Feb. 2012, pp. 1–9.

Oropeza, Lorena, and Dionne Espinoza. *Enriqueta Vasquez and the Chicano Movement: Writings from El Grito del Norte*. Arte Público, 2006.

Padilla, L. M. "But You're Not a Dirty Mexican: Internalized Oppression, Latinos, and Law." *Texas Hispanic Journal of Law and Policy*, no. 7, 2001, pp. 59–113.

Paredes, Américo. *George Washington Gómez*. Arte Público Press, 1990.

Pedraza, Venetia June. *Third Space Mestizaje as a Critical Approach to Literature*. 2008. U of Texas at San Antonio, dissertation. Dissertations and Theses @ University of Texas—San Antonio, ProQuest.

Peña, Lorgia García. *Community as Rebellion: A Syllabus for Surviving Academia as a Woman of Color*. Haymarket Books, 2022.

Pérez, Emma. *The Decolonial Imaginary*. Indiana UP, 1999.

Pérez, Emma. "Irigaray's Female Symbolic in the Making of Chicana Lesbian Sitios y Lenguas (Sites and Discourses)." *Living Chicana Theory*, edited by Carla Trujillo, Third Woman, 1998, pp. 87–101.

Pérez, Loida Maritza. *Geographies of Home*. Penguin Books, 1999.

Pérez-Torres, Rafael. *Mestizaje: Critical Uses of Race in Chicano Culture*. U of Minnesota P, 2006.

Ray, Rashawn, and Alexandra Gibbons. "Why Are States Banning Critical Race Theory?" Brookings Institution, November 2021, www.brookings.edu/articles/why-are-states-banning-critical-race-theory/.

Rendón, Laura. *Sentipensante (Sensing/Thinking) Pedagogy: Educating for Wholeness, Social Justice, and Liberation*. Stylus Publishing, 2008.

Reyhner, Jon Allan, and Jeanne M. Eder. *American Indian Education: A History*. U of Oklahoma P, 2004.

Rideaux, Kia S. "Writing Beyond the Call: One Woman's Response to Gloria Anzaldúa's 'Speaking in Tongues.'" *Global Studies of Childhood*, vol. 7, no. 2, June 2017, pp. 222–28.

Rodriguez, Marc. "A Movement Made of 'Young Mexican Americans Seeking Change': Critical Citizenship, Migration, and the Chicano Movement in Texas and Wisconsin, 1960–1975." *The Western Historical Quarterly*, autumn 2003, pp. 275–99.

Saldívar-Hull, Sonia. *Feminism on the Border: Chicana Gender Politics and Literature*. U of California P, 2000.

Sandoval, Chela. *Methodology of the Oppressed*. U of Minnesota P, 2000.

Sandoval, Chela. "U.S. Third World Feminism: The Theory and Method of Oppositional Consciousness in the Postmodern World." *Genders*, no. 10, 1991, pp. 1–24.

San Miguel, Guadalupe Jr., and Richard R. Valencia. "From the Treaty of Guadalupe Hidalgo to Hopwood: The Educational Plight and Struggle of Mexican Americans in the Southwest." *Harvard Educational Review*, vol. 68, no. 3, 1998, pp. 353–412.

Saragoza, Elvira. "La Mujer in the Chicano Movement." *Chicana Feminist Thought: The Basic Historical Writings*, edited by Alma García, Routledge, 1997, pp. 77–78.

Silverstein, Merril, and Xuan Chen. "The Impact of Acculturation in Mexican American Families on the Quality of Adult Grandchild-Grandparent Relationships." *Journal of Marriage and the Family*, vol. 61, no. 1, 1999, pp. 188–98.

Smith, Andrea. "Boarding School Abuses and the Case for Reparations." *Conquest*, by Smith, South End Press, 2005, pp. 36–54.

Solomon, Dan. "A User's Guide to All the Banned Books in Texas." *Texas Monthly*, 20 Sep. 2022, www.texasmonthly.com/arts-entertainment/users-guide-banned-books-texas.

Solórzano, Daniel G., and Dolores Delgado Bernal. "Examining Transformational Resistance Through a Critical Race and LatCrit Theory Framework." *Urban Education*, no. 3, 2001, pp. 308–36.

Spivak, Gayatri Chakravorty. *The Postcolonial Critic: Interviews, Strategies, Dialogues*. Edited by Sarah Harasym, Routledge, 1990.

State of Arizona, House of Representatives. House Bill 2281. Arizona State Legislature, 2010, www.azleg.gov/legtext/49leg/2r/bills/hb2281s.pdf.

Stephenson, Hank. "What Arizona's 2010 Ban on Ethnic Studies Could Mean for the Fight Over Critical Race Theory." *Politico*, 11 July 2001, www.politico.com/news/magazine/2021/07/11/tucson-unified-school-districts-mexican-american-studies-program-498926.

Tate, Shirley Anne, and Ian Law. "Mixing, *Métissage* and *Mestizaje*." *Caribbean Racisms: Connections and Complexities in the Racialization of the Caribbean Region*, by Tate and Law, Palgrave Macmillan UK, 2015, pp. 50–87. EBSCOhost, doi-org.blume.stmarytx.edu/10.1057/9781137287281_3.

Torres, Edén E. *Chicana Without Apology: The New Chicana Cultural Studies*. Routledge, 2003.

Torres, Vasti. "Bridging Two Worlds: Academia and Latina/o Identity." *The Latina/o Pathway to the Ph.D.: Abriendo Caminos*, edited by Jeanett Castellanos, Alberta M. Gloria, and Mark Kamimura, Taylor and Francis Group, 2006, pp. 135–47.

Treaty of Guadalupe Hidalgo. National Archives, www.archives.gov/milestone-documents/treaty-of-guadalupe-hidalgo. Treaty between Mexico and the United States, signed February 2, 1848 (transcript).

Valencia, Richard R. *Chicano School Failure and Success: Past, Present, and Future*. 2nd ed., Routledge, 2002.

Villenas, Sofia, and Donna Deyhle. "Critical Race Theory and Ethnographies Challenging the Stereotypes: Latino Families, Schooling, Resilience and Resistance." *Curriculum Inquiry*, vol. 29, no. 4, winter 1999, pp. 413–45.

Watford, Tara, Martha A. Rivas, Rebeca Burciaga, and Daniel G. Solórzano. "Latinas and the Doctorate: The 'Status' of Attainment and Experiences from the Margin." *The Latina/o Pathway to the Ph.D.: Abriendo Caminos*, edited by Jeanett Castellanos, Albert M. Gloria, and Mark Kamimura, Taylor and Francis Group, 2006, pp. 113–33.

Weber, David J. *Bárbaros: Spaniards and Their Savages in the Age of Enlightenment*. Hamilton, 2005.

Williams, Raymond. *Keywords: A Vocabulary of Culture and Society*. Revised edition, Oxford UP, 1985.

Yazzie, M. "We Must Make Kin to Get Free: Reflections on #nobansonstoleland in Turtle Island." *Gender, Place, and Culture*, vol. 30, no. 4, 2022, pp. 1–9.

Yellow Bird, Michael. "What We Want to Be Called: Indigenous Peoples' Perspectives on Racial and Ethnic Identity Labels." *American Indian Quarterly*, vol. 23, no. 2, 1999, pp. 1–21.

INDEX

Alberto, Lourdes, 63, 67
Alemán, Enrique, Jr., 41
"Aliens and Others in Search of the Tribe in Academe" (de la tierra), 100, 118
Alvarez, Celia: and academia, 120, 126, 127; and alienation, 120; bilingualism of, 114–15; and class, 117; and cultural community, 117, 120; essay of, 100; and family, 115; and fighting stereotypes, 120; and language, 110, 116, 119; as a Latina, 117, 126; and multiple epistemologies, 108; and multiple identities, 109, 115; privileges of, 118
"Another Way to Grow Up Puerto Rican" (Fiol-Matta), 100, 109
Anzaldúa, Gloria E.: and acculturation, 82, 113; and act of writing, 96, 103, 111–12, 114, 123, 127; and alienation, 82; and belonging, 143; and binary thought, 115; and border culture, 74; and *Borderlands / La Frontera: The New Mestiza*, 68; and bridge image, 48; and Coatlicue state, 75; and *conocimiento* (consciousness), 8, 17, 71, 82, 108, 112, 124–25; and differential consciousness, 124; and earth's environment, 103; and education system, 15n18, 16, 24, 44, 71–72, 87, 110, 112, 126; and empowerment, 103; and "healing the split", 127, 146; and la facultad, 77; and language, 38, 110–12, 132; and literary theory, 144–45; and mestizaje, 63, 64, 66, 68–69, 70, 112; and Mexican American identity, 108; and nepantla (the in-between space), 7–8, 63, 70, 74, 82–83; and new subjectivity, 47, 75, 94; and oppression, 103, 112; poetry of, 110, 111; and Rio Grande Valley, 68; and Spanish language, 38, 110–12, 116; style of, 10, 111–12; theories of, 11, 11n14, 143, 144; and "theory in the flesh", 11; as a third-space feminist, 12, 72; and traumatic experiences, 56, 71–72, 83, 93; and "un arrebato" (jolt), 80; and women of color, 110, 111; and writing from body, 110. *See also Borderlands / La Frontera: The New Mestitza* (Anzaldúa); *This Bridge Called My Back* (Anzaldúa and Moraga)
Arce, Julissa, 49, 56
Austin, Stephen F., 10

Baca, Celeste, 40
Benjamin-Labarthe, Elyette, 39–40

Bernal, Dolores Delgado, 14, 39, 57, 63, 86, 92, 94. *See also Chicana/Latina Education in Everyday Life: Feminista Perspectives on Pedagogy and Epistemology* (Bernal, et al.); education/*educación*
Bhabha, Homi, 7, 72n9
Black Lives Matter, 4, 4n1, 5, 50
Blackwell, Maylei, 39, 44
Bless Me, Ultima (Anaya), 62
book censorship, 4, 5–6, 17, 22n3, 51
Borderlands / La Frontera: The New Mestiza (Anzaldúa) , 7, 10, 11, 13, 15n18, 38, 146. *See also* Anzaldúa, Gloria E.
Brewer, Jan, 50
Brown, Michael, 4n1

Caballero: A Historical Novel (González and Raleigh), 8, 28–34
Cantú, Norma E., 48
Cantú-Sánchez, Margaret, 36n12
Caribbean islands, 64, 69
Castellanos, Jeanett, 57
Castillo, Ana, 66, 67
Castro, Sal, 39
Castro, Vickie, 39
Cervantes, Lorna Dee, 144
Chávez, César, 41
Chicana and Chicano "Pedagogies of the Home" (Guzman-Martinez), 13n16
Chicana feminism, 7, 11–12, 17, 44, 47–48, 57, 107. *See also* education/*educación*; Latina literature
Chicana/Latina Education in Everyday Life: Feminista Perspectives on Pedagogy and Epistemology (Bernal, et al.), 128
¡Chicana Power! (Blackwell), 44
Chicano Youth Liberation Conference, 43
Cisneros, Sandra, 144
City University of New York (CUNY), 120
Clinton, President William Jefferson, 45
Cortés, Hernán, 23
Crisostomo, Paula, 39–40
critical legal theory, 57

critical race theory (CRT), 14, 17, 17n20, 57, 58, 141. *See also* education/*educación*; race
Crockett, Davy, 10
Cullors, Patrisse, 4n1

de la tierra, tatiana, 100, 108–9, 118, 119–21, 126, 127
differential consciousness, 76–77, 87, 90, 91, 107–8, 114. *See also* Anzaldúa, Gloria E.; Lara, Irene; Moraga, Cherríe

education/*educación*: and 2010 census, 50; and "abyssal thinking", 61–62; and acculturation, 86, 101; and affirmative action, 37, 37n13; and African American students, 55, 59n5, 60; and Anglocentric schooling, 7, 7n17, 13, 23, 25, 26–28, 34, 48–49, 50, 57, 60, 64, 66, 75, 84–87, 95, 101, 123, 125, 129, 130; and Asian students, 54; and assimilation, 6–7, 6n5, 10, 11, 14, 15, 18–19, 23, 25, 27, 28, 32, 34, 39, 44, 52, 53, 57, 59, 60, 62, 70, 71, 77, 78, 80, 86–87, 99, 101, 129; and balance, 136, 140; and belonging, 49, 70–71, 77, 84, 102, 130–31, 134, 141, 142; and bilingual education, 42, 48, 59; and binary thought, 61, 62, 70, 76, 82, 84, 92, 101, 102, 107, 112, 118, 145; and BIPOC (Black, Indigenous, and People of Color), 10, 17; and book bans, 22n3, 50, 51; borderlands of, 24; and California, 16n19, 38–39; and caring, 58–59, 85; and censorship, 5, 6–7, 22n3, 51; and Chela Sandoval, 143; and Chicanas, 42–44, 86–87; and Chicana third space feminism, 143, 144; and Chicanxs/Latinxs, 12–13, 16, 34–38, 39–40, 48–49, 111; and class, 16, 35, 35n10, 36, 101, 106, 126; and communities, 52–53, 57, 71, 126; and conflict, 7, 8–9, 11, 13–19, 21, 34, 38, 49, 53, 56, 57, 58, 60, 64, 69, 70, 72, 73, 76, 78, 79, 82, 86, 87, 97, 99, 102–19, 122–27, 128, 130, 132–36, 141, 142;

INDEX

and consciousness, 46–48, 64, 71; and critical race theory (CRT), 17, 17n20, 57, 58, 141, 143; and cultural communities, 128, 143, 146; and cultural education, 4, 14, 73, 138–39; and cultural knowledge, 6, 6n6, 11, 14, 15, 53, 71, 77, 81, 82, 86–87, 128, 137–40; and curriculum, 37, 43, 48–51, 59, 60, 85, 101, 116, 120; deficit model of, 6, 6n6; and DEI (diversity, equity, and inclusion), 5, 49, 50; and discrimination, 6, 6n5, 9, 11, 14, 16n19, 17, 35, 37, 41, 42, 48, 50, 51, 57–58, 60, 77, 80, 98, 127, 131, 141; and docility, 86–87, 100, 101; and doctorates, 37; and Dolores Delgado Bernal, 116, 143; and dropout rates, 54–55; and ethnic studies classes, 116n2, 141; and European White interpretations, 37; and family, 3, 11–12, 13, 14, 52–53, 58, 71, 74, 146; and feminism, 104, 129, 143; and figure of ideal student, 100–101; and financial aid, 44; and formal schooling, 4, 17, 24n6, 53, 82, 140, 145; and gender, 16, 17, 17n20, 35, 80; and GI Bill, 36; and graduation rates, 54, 60, 140, 140n5; and grandparent as *maestra* (teacher), 3, 58; and healing, 127; and higher education, 3, 4, 5, 9, 10–13, 17n20, 19, 28, 34–37, 36n12, 42–46, 49, 50, 51, 53–55, 59, 60, 98, 104, 106, 108–9, 118–23, 125, 127, 128, 130, 134, 137, 139, 145; and high school, 9, 10, 28, 42–44, 48–49, 53–55; history of, 5–6, 10, 16–17, 21, 48; and home, 11, 13n16, 14, 17, 24n6, 58, 77, 129, 137, 139, 140; and immigrants, 48; and inequality, 38–39, 40, 54; interdisciplinary approach to, 141, 144; and K-12 system, 7, 7n8, 9–15, 17, 17n20, 18, 36, 41, 50, 50–52, 59, 60, 62, 70, 97, 98, 105, 110, 125–28, 137; and kinship, 103, 119; and Latinas, 42, 43, 46–48, 52–53, 55–56, 55n3, 57–60, 70–78, 86, 105–9, 122–27; and Latinas/Chicanas, 11, 13–15, 17–19, 21, 24n6, 35n11, 46, 49–50, 59n5, 70–75, 77, 90, 99, 128–30,

145; and Latinos, 35n11, 42, 54, 55n3, 139; and Latinx, 50–58, 64, 101; and Latinx/Chicanx culture, 7n8, 11, 12–18, 52–53, 86–87; and Latinx/Chicanx literature, 5–7, 10, 12, 13, 15, 19, 26–29, 34, 53, 97; and laws, 16–17, 50–51; and life experiences, 58–59, 129; and Mexican Americans, 9–13, 15, 19, 23, 24–25, 26–29, 35–37, 41, 44, 48–50, 57, 128–30, 137, 140, 141; and Native American students, 22, 23, 23n5, 50, 59n5; and oppression, 48, 73, 83, 84, 99, 100, 121, 125, 146; and private schools, 9, 114; and privilege, 125, 126; and racism, 9, 17, 25, 26, 34–36, 39, 44, 48, 50–52, 57, 60, 68–70, 73, 83, 100–3, 106, 110, 111, 120, 122–25, 127, 133, 137; reform of, 43; and rights of Mexicans, 24–25; and school blowouts (walkouts), 39–40, 42; and secondary education, 44; and *sentipensante* pedagogy, 145; and sexism, 39, 44, 46, 48, 70, 77, 99, 100, 102–3, 106, 122, 125; and social justice, 120, 127, 144; and strategic essentialism, 136; and student discourse, 144; and student protests, 39–40, 42; and teachers, 43, 44, 58–59, 60, 85, 87, 100, 111, 115, 131, 132, 142, 143, 145, 146; third space of, 7–8, 11–12, 17, 18, 28–29, 48, 53, 70–72, 74–75, 77–80, 82–84, 90, 92, 98, 102, 104, 105, 107–9, 113–14, 117, 120–21, 123–26, 141, 146; and white students, 54, 55, 60; and Women Authors course, 99, 103, 143; and women of color, 44, 46, 99, 102, 103, 119–20. *See also* El Movimiento (Chicano movement); language; race

"El Corrido de Gregorio Cortez", 12

El Grito del Norte (newspaper), 40

El Movimiento (Chicano movement): and 1969 Denver Youth Conference, 37, 49; and Chicanas, 42–43, 70; and Chicano history, 36–37, 36–37n12, 36n12, 38; and Chicanos, 42, 43; and Chicanx

Indigeneity, 70; and civil rights, 36; and consciousness, 39–40; and discrimination, 36; and equality, 40; and gender, 40; and inclusive pedagogies, 16; and Latinos, 42; and mestizaje concept, 65, 68; and Mexican descent, 36; and multiple identities, 68; and Richard Griswold del Castillo, 36n12; sexism in, 42–43; and Texas, 40–41; women's involvement in, 44; and young organizers, 37

El Plan de Santa Barbara, 37

epistemologies: and Anglocentric epistemologies, 8, 8n11, 15, 30, 49, 73, 80, 90–91, 128, 129; and Anglocentric schooling, 14, 28, 112, 125; and assimilation, 3, 14, 142; and balance, 127, 128, 145; and "banking" system, 18; and binary thought, 60, 61–63, 66; and border culture, 74; and Chicanas, 39, 70, 74–75; and Chicana third space feminism, 47–48, 72; and Chicanxs/Latinxs, 12–16, 17; and communities, 82; and *conocimiento* (consciousness), 18, 75; and cultural epistemologies, 8n11, 19, 21 28–29, 32, 49, 52, 62, 64, 70, 75, 80, 83–84, 86, 90, 95, 96, 102, 106, 107, 109, 125, 127, 144; and differing epistemologies, 3, 4, 8, 28–29, 62, 102, 104, 106, 108–9; and discrimination, 9; and family, 52–53, 142; and gender, 61, 62; and home space, 3, 8n11, 14, 70, 72–73, 81, 82, 124, 127, 141, 142, 145–46; and the "ideal soldier", 18; and Indigenous epistemologies, 22–23, 70, 72; and Latina/Chicana students, 3–4, 8–9, 13–15, 18, 127; and Latinas, 48, 58, 63–64, 73–75; of Latinxs, 8n11, 64, 141; and literature, 64, 93, 94; mestizaje of, 7–9, 14–19, 53, 62–64, 66, 70, 71–73, 74, 76–80, 82, 93, 94, 96–100, 104, 105, 109, 110, 112, 114, 117–21, 123–30, 135–43, 145–46; and Mexican origins, 30; and multiple epistemologies, 81, 83–88, 93, 94, 104, 126–29, 142; and school epistemologies, 9, 14, 64, 70, 72–73, 74, 79, 80, 84, 90, 91, 92, 93, 96, 109, 128–29, 141, 142, 145–46; and *sentipensante* pedagogy, 18, 143; and student protests, 144; and term mestizaje, 8n10; and women of color, 47–48. *See also* differential consciousness

escuelitas (schools), 25, 25n7

European conquest, 21–23, 23n4

Fanon, Franz, 32, 33

Fiol-Matta, Liza: and assimilation, 116, 118; essay of, 100; experiences of, 114, 115–18; family of, 115, 116, 118; and language, 110, 115–16; and multiple epistemologies, 108, 127; and multiple identities, 109, 127; privileges of, 118; as a Puerto Rican, 109, 115–16, 117, 118

Floyd, George, 4–5, 4n1, 50

Foucault, Michel, 18, 34, 86, 87, 100, 101

Friere, Paulo, 18, 96, 122

Garcia, Gina Ann, 45, 46, 46n17, 54

Garcia, Mario T., 36, 36n12, 44, 48

Garcia, Teresa, 36

Garner, Eric, 4n1

Garza, Alicia, 4n1

Geographies of Home (Pérez), 69, 146

George Washington Gómez (Paredes), 8, 11, 15, 26–29, 28, 34

Golondrina, Why Did You Leave Me? (González), 90–91; and agency, 92; and alienation, 79, 82, 84, 85, 86; Amada Garcia in, 79–82, 87–90, 93, 96; and Anglocentric epistemologies, 89, 90–91; and assimilation, 84, 86, 91; and belonging, 84, 86; and binary thought, 97; and *conocimiento* (consciousness), 80, 93, 94, 96; dances in, 95–96, 97; and empowerment, 92; and family, 80, 81, 82, 84–95, 96, 97; and female bonding, 95; and golondrina (swallow) legend, 81n1; and identity, 56, 79, 80, 84, 85–94, 96, 97; and *india* blood, 88; and language,

85–86, 87, 90–91; and Latinas/Chicanas, 12, 56, 85, 88, 90–91, 97, 146; and Lucero, 18, 69, 78, 79, 80–97, 98; and maternal knowledge, 81, 87; and Mexican Americans, 84–90, 93, 95, 96; and Native American heritage, 88; and nepantla (the in-between space), 82–84, 91; and oppression, 86, 92; and *sentipensante* pedagogy, 91; storytelling in, 89–97; and strategic essentialism, 91–92; and third space, 93; and traumatic experiences, 80, 84; and U.S. education system, 11, 84–86; and women's roles, 91

González, Barbara Renaud, 11, 12, 18, 56, 79, 81. *See also* Latina literature

González, Jovita, 8, 10

healing, 73, 75, 97, 100, 103, 119, 146. *See also* Anzaldúa, Gloria E.; identities; Lara, Irene

"Healing Sueños for Academia" (Lara), 100

Hernandez v. Driscoll CISD, 41

Hispanic Association of Colleges and Universities, 45

Hispanic-serving institutions (HSIs), 12, 45–46, 45n15, 46n16, 54

House on Mango Street, The (Cisneros), 10, 146

Hurtado, Aída, 57, 106

hybridity, 72n9

I Am Not Your Perfect Mexican Daughter (Sánchez), 49

identities: and acceptance of self, 127; and Afro-mestizaje cultures, 68, 70; and alienation, 27, 53, 56, 62, 66, 86, 117, 142; and American identity, 28–29; and Anglo identity, 68, 130, 131; and assimilation, 14, 25, 28, 32, 33, 62, 72, 124, 125, 136; and balance, 124, 125; and belonging, 81–82, 136; and binary thought, 64, 71, 72, 96, 125–26; and border culture, 74; and Chicana identity, 38, 39, 49, 65, 67, 68, 71–72, 75–76, 92, 96, 122; and Chicanxs, 65, 67, 68; and class, 61, 62, 71, 72; and colonization, 65–66; and communal ties, 79, 102, 126, 127, 129, 143; and conflict, 7, 11, 15–18, 25, 28–30, 49, 56, 58, 66, 73, 106, 111, 114, 122, 133–34; and *conocimiento* (consciousness), 8–9, 8n12, 15, 49, 63, 64, 73, 75–77, 83; and cultural identities, 8, 12–16, 18, 24–25, 27–28, 38, 49, 64, 65, 71, 81, 102, 111, 112, 118, 123, 129, 130, 136–38, 142, 145; and cultural knowledge, 140–41, 145; and decolonial imaginary, 15, 75–76; and discrimination, 14, 122n3; and empowerment, 127; and ethnic identity, 120, 122–23; and family, 14, 15, 17, 53, 56, 61, 79; and feminism, 72, 76; forgetting of, 142; and gender, 30, 32, 61, 62, 71; and Hispanics, 130, 131, 132, 137; and holistic identity, 121; and identity politics, 91, 92, 108; and Indigenous identities, 16, 23, 61, 65, 66–71, 88, 124; and individual/communal binary, 61, 72n9; and intermarriage with Anglo men, 29, 30–34; and internalized racism, 121–22, 136; and language, 38, 67n8; and Latina/Chicana students, 3–4, 7–8, 14–18, 61, 72–73; and Latinas, 53, 55–58, 61–63, 66–69, 75–76, 92, 98, 116, 117, 124–25; and Latinx/Chicanx students, 38; and Latinx identities, 16, 17, 38; and literature, 4, 8, 12, 18, 26–34, 55–56, 80; and mestizaje, 63–73, 75–76, 88–89, 93, 96–97; and Mexican Americans, 28–29, 30, 67, 68, 80, 93, 108, 131, 132; and Mexican identity, 68, 82, 116n2; and multiple identities, 73, 80–82, 87, 92, 97, 113–16, 121, 122, 124, 126; and nationality, 71; and Native American identity, 7n9, 66–67; and nepantla (the in-between space), 73–74; and oppression, 50, 62, 70, 77–78, 80, 113, 114; and Puerto Rican identity, 115, 120; reconstruction of, 96; and religion, 62; and Spanish identity,

68; and stereotypes, 120, 121, 124; of students, 143; and traumatic experiences, 77, 125; and women of color, 118–21. *See also* Chicana feminism

immigration, 36, 50, 56, 60, 88, 116n2, 130

Indigenous peoples: and acculturation, 22; and assimilation, 22, 67; and Aztecs, 21, 22; and book burning, 22–23; in Canada, 21n1; and Chicanas, 66–67; and cultural genocide, 22; and education, 22–23; and Incas, 21, 22; and Latinas, 66–67; and Mayans, 21, 22; and mestizaje, 66–67; and Mexicans, 22–23; names of, 133; and North American tribes, 21; as servants, 30; and Spanish control, 65; and term *mestizaje*, 65; violence against, 56; and women, 107. *See also* Native Americans

Injustice Never Leaves You: Anti-Mexican Violence in Texas (Martinez), 25

intersectionality, 44, 46, 48, 99

Irigaray, Luce, 91, 92

Kauffman, Albert H., 57
Keys, Alicia, 5n2

"La Feminista" (Nieto-Gómez), 44
"La Güera" (Moraga), 100, 109, 112–14
language: and bilingual education, 42, 48, 59, 114, 116–17n2; and bilingual students, 116, 130; and *Bridge* anthology, 110; and caló, 119; and code-switching, 146; and conflict, 142; and connection to culture, 131, 132, 145; and discrimination, 110, 131–32; and English language, 27, 38, 41, 57–58, 59, 61–62, 82, 84, 85, 86, 87, 88, 90–91, 97, 106, 108–12, 114, 115, 116, 118, 119, 130, 132; forgetting of, 142; and Indigenous people, 21n1, 22; and language barriers, 60, 85; and language difficulties, 36, 41, 84; and Latinas/Chicanas, 18, 38, 60, 72, 74, 106, 109–14; and law, 17n20, 41; and mestizaje, 63, 112; and metaphor, 73; and retaining native language, 15, 38, 86, 106, 109, 110–12, 116;

in school setting, 109–12, 116; and segregation, 57–58; and Spanglish, 38, 112, 130; and Spanish language, 14, 25, 27, 38, 61–62, 69, 82, 84, 85, 86, 87, 88, 90, 106, 108, 110–12, 114, 115, 116, 118, 119, 130–32; and spelling of *Chicana/o* as *Xicana/o*, 67, 67n8; and storytelling, 90. *See also* mispronunciation of names; "Speaking in Tongues: A Letter to Third World Women Writers" (Anzaldúa)

Lara, Irene: and academia, 119–20, 123, 124, 126, 127; and alienation, 119; and college classes, 108–9; and cultural knowledge, 119, 120; and differential consciousness, 124; and healing, 123; and internalized racism, 121; and language, 119, 123; mixed-race ancestry of, 119, 123, 124; and multiple epistemologies, 108, 123, 127; and *sentipensante* pedagogy, 119; and spirituality, 119–20, 124; and writing, 123

La Raza (newspaper), 40

La Raza Unida conference, 41–42

Latina Feminist Group, 104, 137

Latina literature: and Afro-Latina protagonists, 69; and Barbara Gonzalez, 144; and Chicana third space feminism, 58, 141; and the Chicana writer, 145; and common words, 142; and communities, 78, 143; and critical race theory (CRT), 58; and Dominican Americans, 69; and empowerment, 75, 143; and family, 78; and feminism, 99, 128; and fiction, 104; and knowledge, 94, 142–43, 145; lack of, 125; and Native American women, 145; and Puerto Ricans, 69, 109, 115; reading of, 74, 75, 143, 144–45; and students, 143; and theories, 57, 78, 144–45; and women of color, 78, 99, 110, 111, 143, 144–45. *See also* Anzaldúa, Gloria E.; education/*educación*; *Golondrina, Why Did You Leave Me?* (González); Moraga, Cherríe; *testimonios* (testimonies)

Latin America, 64–65

Lemon Grove case, 11

LGBTQIA+ people: and book banning, 17; and book content, 51; and discrimination, 5, 17n20; and lesbians, 113, 118, 121; and queer people, 126; and sexual identification, 5n3
Lorde, Audre, 46

MacDonald, Victoria-Maria, 35–36, 37, 44, 45, 48
Martin, Trayvon, 4n1
Mendez, Lupe, 13
Mendez v. Westminster, 11
Mestizaje: Critical Uses of Race in Chicano Culture (Pérez-Torres), 65
Mexican American Legal Defense and Education Fund, 57
Mexican-American War, 8, 9, 23, 24, 26, 28
Mexican American Youth Leadership Conference, 39
Mexican American Youth Organization, 41, 42
Mexico: and Amada Garcia, 90; and citizenship, 24; and immigrants, 60, 116n2; and Native identities, 67; northern region of, 35; and U.S.-Mexican border, 8, 48, 74, 79, 81
Mignolo, Walter, 73
mispronunciation of names, 132–34, 136
Monzó, Lilia D., 58
Moraga, Cherríe: and academia, 123, 126, 127; and binary thought, 115, 121; and *Bridge* anthology, 56, 99; as a Chicana, 67, 108, 113, 114, 121; and differential consciousness, 124; and empowerment, 103; and feminists of color, 99; and Indigenous identity, 67; and language, 110, 112, 116, 132; and multiple epistemologies, 108, 114, 127; and new subjectivity, 47, 113; and oppression, 122; poetry of, 113; and privilege, 112–13, 114, 118, 135; and racism, 108, 121–22, 135; theories of, 11, 144; as a third-space feminist, 12; and traumatic experiences, 112; and writing, 114, 123. See also "La Güera" (Moraga)

Mount, Tanya Luna, 40
Muñoz, Carlos, 37

Native Americans, 22, 23, 50, 56, 59n5, 66–67. See also *Golondrina, Why Did You Leave Me?* (González)

Paredes, Américo, 8, 10, 26, 27, 28
Peña, Lorgia Garcia, 102
Pérez, Emma: and assimilation, 15n18; and Chicana history, 89, 106–7; and decolonial imaginary, 17–18, 75–76, 107; and "herstories", 124; theories of, 143
Pérez, Loida Maritza, 144
Pérez-Torres, Rafael, 63, 65–66

race: and Africans, 65, 68–69, 70, 133; and Anglocentrism, 137; and antiracist pedagogies, 19, 68; and assimilation, 65, 78; and belonging, 130–31; and BIPOC (Black, Indigenous, and People of Color), 5–6, 5n3, 6n5; and California Proposition 209, 16, 16n19; and caste society, 65; and Celia Alvarez, 117; and censorship, 5, 6–7; and citizenship, 69; and college degrees, 35; and college enrollments, 55; as a construct, 66; and critical race theory (CRT), 14, 17, 17n20, 50; and cultural conflict, 136; and DEI (diversity, equity, and inclusion), 59; and discrimination, 4–6, 4n1, 5n3, 17, 37, 48, 50, 51, 122n3; and Dominican Republic, 69–70; and education, 75, 80, 84, 85, 98; and education system, 129; and ethnic studies classes, 50; and feminism, 47, 48, 129; and health disparities, 4; and hierarchies, 69; and Indigenous people, 21n1; and interracial marriage, 25; and Irene Lara, 119; and *"la raza"*, 40, 41–42, 64; and literature, 5–6, 50; and mestizaje, 64–70; and Mexican Americans, 134–35; and microaggressions, 136; and mispronouncing names, 133–34; and "Mixing, Metissage and Mestizaje" (Law and Tate), 69; and NAACP chapters, 5; and police violence, 4, 50; and politics, 25–26; and racial identity, 21–22n1, 69–70; and racial inequities, 4–6; and racism, 9, 17, 24, 26–27, 32, 36, 37, 39, 50–51, 57, 60, 66, 68, 69, 70, 77, 80, 84, 92, 103, 134–35; and racist laws, 50; and racist pedagogies, 16, 39, 59; and renaming, 133; and segregation, 69; and skin color, 88, 112–13, 134–35; and slavery, 60, 65, 69, 133; and social justice, 124; and society, 129; and Spanish ancestry, 36; and Spanish colonization, 64–65, 69; and students of color, 133–34; and systemic racism, 101; and terms *Chicanx and Latinx*, 6n4; and white superiority, 65, 69; and women of color, 82. *See also* education/*educación*; Indigenous peoples

Rendón, Laura, 15n18, 18, 58–59, 60, 85, 91, 142, 143–44. *See also* education/*educación*

Rodriguez, Celia Herrera, 67

Rueda, Robert S., 58

Saldívar-Hull, Sonia, 144

Sandoval, Chela, 15n18, 18, 63, 74, 76–77, 90, 107–8. *See also* education/*educación*

Santa Anna, 9

Selena (movie), 13

Sentipensante (Sensing/Thinking) Pedagogy (Rendón), 15n18, 58–59

sexuality: and binary thought, 101, 107; and education, 75, 126; and heterosexuals, 101, 107, 126, 130; and identity, 62, 113; and inequality, 71; and lesbians, 113, 118, 121; and nationalist projects, 68; and queerness, 72, 101, 107, 126; and sexual identification, 61, 119. *See also* LGBTQIA+ people

"Snapshots from my Daze in School" (Alvarez), 100, 109

Solórzano, Daniel, 143

Somos MAS, 12

Spain, 65

"Speaking in Tongues: A Letter to Third World Women Writers" (Anzaldúa), 100, 109, 110, 111–12

St. Mary's University, 12, 41, 140

Telling to Live: Latina Feminist Testimonios (Latina Feminist Group), 9, 18, 56, 98, 99, 104, 109. *See also testimonios* (testimonies)

testimonios (testimonies): analysis of, 7, 18, 106, 127; and assimilation, 10, 137; and communal solidarity, 135–36; and consciousness, 105, 135–36; and context of term, 9n13; and cultural communities, 98, 99, 102, 105; and cultural conflict, 130–39; definition of, 104, 105; and discrimination, 135, 136, 137; and education testimonios, 56, 98, 99, 102, 104–7, 110, 126, 127, 130; of Generation Z, 49; and identities, 99, 107; and individual/collective binary, 105; and Latinas, 53, 55–58, 64, 74, 97, 98–101, 105; and Latinas/Chicanas, 13, 14, 18, 19, 105, 107; and Latinx literature, 49, 130; and marginalized peoples, 105; and microaggressions, 132–34; and oppression, 101–2, 105; and sharing of experiences, 126; of students, 9, 19, 127–35; and *Telling to Live: Latina Feminist Testimonios*, 105, 106, 142; and *This Bridge* anthologies, 104, 105, 106, 142, 143

Texas: and anti-diversity, equity and inclusion laws, 50–51; anti-Mexican violence in, 25, 28; and assimilation, 28; Austin in, 41; book censorship in, 17; and border with Mexico, 48; Brownsville in, 10, 48; and Chicanx/Latinx students, 42, 143; and colonization, 22n3, 28; and critical race theory (CRT), 50; and Crystal City, 42; curricula in, 12, 59n4; and Dr. Hector P. Garcia, 41; and *Golondrina, Why Did you Leave Me?*, 79, 82, 93; and history, 9–10, 28; Laredo in, 48; and Mexican American students, 57; and Mexican American studies, 59n4, 141; and Mexican army, 28; movimiento in, 40, 41; public education in, 19, 40–41, 42, 50–51, 57, 60, 127; and Rio Grande Valley schools, 40–41; and San Antonio, 9, 12, 42, 134, 137; and south Texas, 41, 42; standardized testing in, 59; and student protests, 16, 42; and systemic racism, 127; and Texas Mexicans, 24, 26, 27, 28; and Texas Rangers, 8, 26, 30; University of, 41; Uvalde in, 42

This Bridge Called My Back (Anzaldúa and Moraga), 12, 18, 47–48, 56, 98, 99, 102–4, 109. *See also testimonios* (testimonies)

This Bridge We Call Home: Radical Visions for Transformation (Anzaldúa and Keating), 18, 47, 56, 98, 99, 103, 104, 109. *See also testimonios* (testimonies)

Tometi, Ayo, 4n1

Torres, Edén E., 43–44, 56

Treaty of Guadalupe Hidalgo, 8, 24–25, 26, 28, 88

Trump, Donald, 4, 17n20

United Farm Workers Organizing Committee, 41

United States: and 2010 census, 55n3; and acculturation, 81–82; and African Americans, 68, 69; Alabama in, 17, 116n2; and the Alamo, 9–10, 27; as *America*, 22n2; and Arizona, 17, 48, 50, 116n2, 140n5; and Asian voters, 133; and assimilation, 49, 56–57; Black Power movement in, 117; book bans in, 4, 5–6, 50–51; and border with Mexico, 8, 24, 74, 79, 81; California in, 16, 37, 38–39, 40, 59; and Chicanas/Latinas, 92; and Chicanxs, 11, 67; citizenship in, 23–24, 26; and colonization, 24, 67; Colorado Springs in, 115; and *The Condition of Education for Hispanic Americans*, 45; Constitution of, 24; and COVID-19 pandemic, 4–5, 50, 54, 60, 143; and Denver, Colorado, 43; and discrimination, 4–6, 36; education system in, 5–7, 6n5, 8, 11, 13–17, 15n18, 18, 19, 21–24, 26–27, 34, 36, 44–46, 48–53, 57, 58–62, 59n5, 63, 73–76, 82, 90, 93, 96, 100, 101, 105, 125, 127–29, 141, 145; farmworkers in, 41; and feminism, 46–48, 107–8; and Florida, 5, 17, 17n20, 22n3, 27n9, 50–51; and GI Bill, 35, 36; Hawaii in, 89; and health care system, 5; Jim Crow era in, 5, 25; and Juan Crow laws, 25; and Latinx population, 54; and Latinxs, 11, 23, 44–46, 48–58, 67; laws in, 4, 5, 6, 25, 37n13, 50–51, 116n2; and Mexican Americans, 11, 23–30, 35–37, 39, 56, 67, 80; and Mexican land, 24, 28; minorities of color in, 5n2; Mississippi in, 17; Missouri in, 4n1; New York in, 4n1; Oklahoma in, 17, 17n20, 27n9, 88; poverty in, 80; protests in, 16, 42, 50; and Puerto Rico, 116, 120; and rights of Mexicans, 25–26; and South Carolina, 115; South of, 19, 25; Southwest of, 16, 22, 25, 28, 41, 88; and systemic racism, 4–5, 4n1, 9, 17, 57; and Texas, 5–7, 9, 19, 22n3, 27n9, 28, 40–41, 50, 57, 59, 127, 134; and violence against Mexicans, 8, 28; and War on Poverty programs, 41; and women of color, 62–63, 108. *See also* immigration; Texas

University of California, 37

Valenzuela, Angela, 6n6

Vasquez, Enriqueta, 40

Walkout (Olmos), 39

We Are Here movement, 5, 5n2

Yazzie, Melanie K., 103

You Sound Like a White Girl (Arce), 49

ABOUT THE AUTHOR

Margaret Cantú-Sánchez is a visiting instructor of English at St. Mary's University, teaching composition and multiethnic and Latinx literature. Her research focuses on Chicanx feminist theories, decolonizing pedagogies, immigration, and border studies. Her publications include approaches to teaching Latinx literature, examination of contemporary Latinx literature, and applications of Chicana third-space feminist theories. She is the co-editor of *Teaching Gloria E. Anzaldúa*, which offers inspiring ideas for the classroom and community utilizing Anzaldúa's theories and concepts.